The 28th Amendment

The 28th Amendment

Who is the Village Idiot?

N.O. Slak

iUniverse, Inc.
New York   Bloomington

The 28th Amendment
Who is the Village Idiot?

iUniverse books may be ordered through booksellers or by contacting:

iUniverse
1663 Liberty Drive
Bloomington, IN 47403
www.iuniverse.com
1-800-Authors (1-800-288-4677)

Because of the dynamic nature of the Internet, any Web addresses or links contained in this book may have changed since publication and may no longer be valid. The views expressed in this work are solely those of the author and do not necessarily reflect the views of the publisher, and the publisher hereby disclaims any responsibility for them.

ISBN: 978-1-4502-1400-1 (SOFT)
ISBN: 978-1-4502-1399-8 (HARD)
ISBN: 978-1-4502-1398-1 (EBOOK)

Library of Congress Control Number: 2010902532

Printed in the United States of America

iUniverse rev. date: 3/10/2010

<u>Author's Disclaimer:</u> I'm only an expert in a few subjects, but have an opinion for anything that can be discussed. If I offended the living, the dead or even the people that perish while this book is in its third reprint, it was not intentional. If I offended, defamed, hurt or accidentally maimed anybody, it was not me, but my evil twin brother.

I would like to thank Bing, Google, and Wikipedia for their valuable assistance.

This is a political satire and is not to be confused with a dictionary, encyclopedia, or bodies of work that are factual or intellectual. That should cover my behind. However, if people feel they were a victim of a malicious attack, I will send them a fruit basket. The fruit basket will be hand delivered by Mike Tyson. If Mike is not available, then my promise becomes broken.

If our politicians can lie, cheat, and steal, then nobody should take offense to this book, except for people with dyslexia. My advice to those unfortunate souls is to turn the book upside down and read it in a mirror.

WWW.NOSLAK.com

By: N.O. Slak

Previous literary classics by N.O. Slak include The American Nutcracker, Time for some old school crackin' and The Rebel of the Asylum; I played their game my way.

Contents

INTRODUCTION

As we all know, Sarah Palin resigned as the Governor of Alaska. I think it is terrible what the media, her colleagues, and even the GOP said about her and her family. The unsolicited comments by David Letterman were not funny at all. Nevertheless, nothing he says makes me laugh. I find his sense of humor as funny as an oxygen bottle.

That's Jon Stewart's competition! No wonder he wins the Emmy every year. He has to contend against Bill Maher, Conan O'Brien, SNL, etc. Gee, where's my stage. I contend that most Special Olympians could beat his competition. Stewart does a good job of hiding his personal political affiliation on the show, although I would safely bet he leans to the left. However, his approach to making fun of both sides is rather refreshing.

It was a sad day in my life when Sarah announced her resignation. She is a good-looking woman, smart and full of life. From my perspective, most of our female politicians look like lumberjack lesbians and don't have much to add to the further development of our country. There are more stupid male politicians than women, but I don't stare at men the same as I do as women. I turn my head when Barney Frank bends over to pick up something.

It was not until I saw the professorial and liver-lipped looking Charlie Gibson's feeble attempt to grill Sarah Palin like a piece of flank steak that I realized it is time for this country to have a new dogma. I vividly recall Gibson's interview of Sarah on September 11, 2008 and I heard the dumbest question asked by Charlie.

I do not think he realized his own question was going to stir the nation and receive as much publicity as Michael Jackson's recent demise. The media chose to play the infamous question and answer more often during the month of September than Keith Richards brushed his teeth in the entire year. Other than her recent term of *death panel,* she has never garnered so much publicity from an interview.

Gibson: "Do you agree with the Bush doctrine?"

Palin: "In what respect Charlie?" Gibson sat there like a deer looking at oncoming traffic and his glasses started to steam.

Gibson: "The Bush—well, what do you—what do you interpret it to be?"

Palin: "His world view"- *Great answer Sarah!*

Gibson: "No, the Bush doctrine, enunciated September 2002, before the Iraq war."

Palin: "I believe that what President Bush has attempted to do is rid this world of Islamic extremism, terrorists who are hell-bent on destroying our nation. There have been blunders along the way, though. There have been mistakes made. With new leadership, and that's the beauty of American elections, of course and democracy, is with new leadership comes opportunity to do things better."

Gibson: "The Bush doctrine, as I understand it, is that we have the right of anticipatory self-defense, that we have the right to a preemptive strike against any country that we think is going to attack us. Do you agree with that?"

Palin :-(Should have said) "Damn right I do, you pathetic little jackal. I believe Clinton launched a major military intervention in Kosovo without UN approval. Do you take this crap seriously Charlie? I have a Colt-45 strapped to my thigh and I am ready to pull it out and crack your pea-brain sized melon. Quit asking me silly questions. I already told you my cup-size, but I'm not going to sit here all day listening to your asinine questions anymore."

Sarah, please stick to your convictions and stay the course. I would rather have a woman with common sense, not to mention one who hunts, as our next Commander-in- Chief. If you get a chance to email me, make sure to set a date for us to go fishing. Naturally, I expect to meet the rest of the family, because a fish fry for two is boring. We have them in the trailer park almost every Friday night in the summer months. Fish, Pabst Blue Ribbon and stories about our current elected officials would make for an extremely funny, yet delightful evening.

We could spend hours talking about how you would manage the senior citizens that are now running our country. If Strom Thurmond were alive, I could tell you so many jokes! However, as my mother always told me, it is not nice to make fun of the dead. Nevertheless, do not let it get you down, because I have more Nancy Pelosi jokes than a midget has neck aches. I am looking forward to the invite.

PS Use the screen name Alaskanbabe, so my agent knows it is you. This will make it easier on the poor sap, because as you know, I get thousands of emails a day. As usual, I will bring the beer, but don't expect me to bring $63,500.

We need an all-encompassing doctrine, not just one that applies to our country's direction towards military threats. We survived the Monroe, Bush, Regan and even Clinton's doctrine, which was to leave no girl left behind. However, we never had one that stood timeless. As we continue to watch our country slip into the abyss, now is the perfect time to unleash the ultimate dogma.

We need a doctrine written and executed. It should be an overall amendment to our constitution. Part of our problem is the ages of our current Chief Justices! Justice John Roberts, Jr. must feel like he is working in a geriatrics ward. If Gidget is only sixty-three and hawking Boniva for osteoporosis, then I am surprised we do not hear the Justices' bones shatter when they walk to their bench. I don't wish any ill will towards anybody, but how much longer can Justice Ruth Ginsburg drag out her current condition? She claims she enjoys the opera, and there is no reason to disbelieve her. She could have seen Cleopatra, as well as had dinner with her.

Our new doctrine should reflect the appropriate changes to our first amendment as well as deter fat people from thinking they have rights. Other than getting most of their information from the back of menus, where in our constitution does it say that our fat and sweaty citizens have special rights? They should have the right to two helpings at a smorgasbord, but that is about it. If fat people don't like paying for two seats on an airplane, then I suggest they put their forks down. My God, they do not realize my life is in jeopardy if I have the middle seat during a long distance flight. I could drown in their puddle of sweat, not to mention suffer from fractured ribs if one of them was to fall asleep and lean into me.

Where are my rights? Where have the rights gone for the majority? I'm not supposed to say Merry Christmas anymore, because it's considered politically taboo, yet I do. This country's foundation is for the majority, not the vocal minority. If anybody thinks for one nanosecond that I care about the freaks who believe in Scientology, they need to snap out of their coma. In addition, our constitution is for the people and not animals. Somebody needs to remind PETA that most people do not mimic Michael Vick.

Now that our nation has elected Obama as our commander in chief, the democrats have really put their necks on the line. The majority of our voters bypassed the proverbial branch and went straight to the twig on the American tree. Therefore, time is of the essence to have our new dogma in place before it becomes worse. There are too many issues on our plate involving foreign affairs, our economy and more important subject matters than having to listen to a PETA-puppet. This new dogma will address freedom of speech, smokers' rights and a cornucopia of other topics that we need to adopt in my newly proposed amendment.

If I can quote one of our greatest presidents, it would be Abraham Lincoln. He was at least attributed to saying, "You can fool some of the people all of the time, and you can fool all of the people some of the time, but you can't fool all of the people all of the time." I wonder if he was clairvoyant, because he must have seen into the future. Although that catchy phrase is not the written credo of a lot of SIG's (special interest groups) it sure does appear that is how they are running their shows. PT Barnum would be proud and Siegfried and Roy would blush at the amount of hypocrisy and greed that is happening in America.

We are a nation that has evolved into letting every tribe have a say-so in all aspects of everyday living. Speaking of tribes, even our Native Americans are reaping the benefits through their casinos. That proves that good things happen to those who are beat into submission, but it has nothing to do with the Kabala-worshiping fruitcakes. People from the Volunteer State should never complain. They volunteered to help Andrew Jackson in the battle of New Orleans, but did not volunteer to pick cotton.

This newly proposed doctrine would reinstate and reconfirm that the Republican Party is not dead. Republicans don't need a Tea Party to get in the way. The only thing the Tea Party is good for is making me realize that the Republican Party lost their focus and took their eye of the prize. The far-right lunatic fringe is just as scary as the far-left. The Republicans need to realign their troops and get ready to do battle in 2011, but it doesn't stand a chance now. Did Abraham Lincoln speak about gay rights, abortion, and the rights for fat slobs when he ran for president?

President Lincoln wasn't even on the ballots of 10 states in the south, yet still defeated Douglas. At this very moment, too many people argue who had more pressure on them, Bush Jr. or Obama, but it's a wasted argument. Lincoln successfully defused the Trent Affair, beat the secessionists in the confederate states and managed his own reelection! He didn't have Ron Howard make him a video to help rally the ignorant to vote. He didn't have lobbyists, Oprah or greasy snake-oil salesmen shoving him into office.

In his famous 1858 speech upon acceptance of his nomination, he said, "A house divided against itself cannot stand." We are a broken nation of false and empty promises. We have perpetuated ourselves into the land of beer summits and stupid legislation. If Lincoln were alive today, he would go to war again, however it would be to help states wishing to secede for the sole purpose to live their lives free from congressional imbeciles.

If we don't adopt this new doctrine, we might as well put our country up for sale, because it proves we no longer care. Moreover, it will prove we lost our way along the road to greatness. The timing is right to give our nation a new doctrine, aptly titled *the 28th Amendment.*

Freedom of Speech

It appears we are losing our freedom of speech, which is one of our most cherished rights. The root cause of this is due to the media and political correctness. Although some people make comments that may offend others, there is no reason to have stories whipped into a froth like an overpriced latte at Starbucks. We must maintain our beloved freedom at all costs and quit listening to people who feel they were a *victim* of a comment. Ask a person in a burn-unit what's more painful, their injury or listening to Al Sharpton defending a victim of an alleged racial slur. That may be an unfair question, because both are equally as painful and ugly.

Certain groups do not want normal people to use the word God, let alone see His name in writing. Yet, these same people do not mind spending US currency. Other people have chosen their life's work to defend alleged racial remarks or make it their duty to ruin my Christmas. These types of people annoy me like a rash growing on an open wound.

One of the biggest gripes by the minority of citizens in this country is to have the name God stricken from anywhere it appears. The ACLU wants it removed from public schools and cites the constitution as its argument. Atheists want the word God removed, but they are not sure who to blame or how to argue their logic. I want the ACLU to disappear, not God.

The word God does not appear in our constitution, yet His name is in the Declaration of Independence. It states, "Laws of Nature and Nature's God entitled." The same document states, "We hold these truths to be self evident, that all men are created equal, that they are endowed by their *creator* with certain unalienable rights, that among these are life, liberty, and the pursuit of happiness." It ends by stating, "And for the support of this Declaration, with a firm reliance on the protection of *divine providence*, we mutually pledge to each other our lives, our fortunes and our *sacred honor.*"

Where does it say the words, monkey, flying saucer, or any other idol that some people prefer to worship? Do our far-left friends and other lunatics understand the words *divine providence?* Yet, the beautiful part about our country is anybody can worship what he or she wants. If you want to pray to a tree, monkey, or even a wrench, then knock yourself out. I do not care what anybody believes in spiritually, yet I wish the vocal minority would keep their whining to a minimum.

God is not in our constitution, but neither are the words, *Separation of Church and State.* Those words do not appear in any amendment or our constitution, but you get an earful of that crap everyday, do you not? The people that whine about us having the word God on our money are the same imbeciles who would cash the winning lottery ticket faster than light propulsion.

The term Separation of Church and State came from a twisted US Supreme Court ruling in1947. The name of the infamous case was Everson v Board of Education of Ewing Twp., New Jersey. Everson thought his taxes should not have to support buses transporting children to a Christian school and the court decided by a 5-4 vote to rule in his favor. Interestingly, we had a previous KKK member, Hugo Black; author the opinion for the court.

This Justice was all over the map like a blue-line on several of his opinions, let alone this one. Justices Jackson and Rutledge authored far more compelling and eloquent dissents. Do you think Justice Black was on narcotics, when he wrote, "The establishment of religion clause of the First Amendment means at least this" and then proceeds to author his opinion as though it were fact?

Everson v Board of Education was nothing more than a disgruntled taxpayer, yet the court's decision opened Pandora's Box. My taxes not only help to pay for school buses, both the long and short versions, but also city buses, airport buses, prison buses, special needs buses, transit buses and even VIP buses. Do you hear me whining Everson? Hello, where are you Everson? I do not know if he is alive or dead, but so far, he has not yelled back. Perhaps somebody shoved him in front of a bus.

We would be doing ourselves a service by not listening to the constant snivelers about what normal people say. We are politically incorrect if we say Merry Christmas as opposed to Happy Holidays, because we may infringe on others' beliefs. Some city officials started banning Christmas trees in public places.

The City Manager of Eugene Oregon did this in the year 2000 citing *separation of church and state.* I already knew Oregon was a den of iniquity, because it borders California, but what was this person thinking? Is he an interpreter of the Constitution as well? In fact, it has become so ridiculous; we call Christmas trees Holiday trees. A pine tree adorned with lights and ornaments standing in or outside of a structure around the December time period is a Christmas tree! Notwithstanding, approximately 76% of our population are Christians, but if you include the Mormons, then it would be 78%, or 225 million people.

There are approximately four million people, or 1.3% of the population who celebrate Judaism. I do not call their Menorah a Holiday candle.

The 1.3 million atheists are probably just glad to see twinkling lights on a Christmas tree in any town and pray they will see another one the following year.

There are approximately 2-million Mormons. The men probably have two of their wives cut down the Christmas tree, while they drink whisky and coffee, and give one of their daughter's friends a well-needed rest.

The 1.4million Agnostics acknowledge a tree with twinkling lights, but they have no personal knowledge of how it got there.

The 78,000 Scientologists are miffed, because I think the FAA put a ban on lit Christmas trees inside spaceships while in flight.

The 875,000 Unitarians huddle in amazement at the sight of a beautifully adorned Christmas tree. They are not sure which God to thank.

I do not care how you do the math; it is overwhelmingly acceptable to call a Christmas tree a Christmas tree. No matter what the percentages are, people are always going to upset somebody, but I personally do not care and why should I? The math proves the majority of people in the US believes in Christmas, but is afraid to offend others accidentally. Based on religious statistics, there is only a one in ten chance that you will annoy someone and I will take those odds any day.

Furthermore, why do companies promote Holiday Parties, yet have a Christmas tree? I have never been to a company sanctioned *Holiday Party*, where I saw a Christmas tree, Menorah, spaceship, monkey and a separate table adorned with a Kwanzaa candle. Most importantly, if I wish someone a Merry Christmas and he or she responds by saying, "Happy Holidays", I do not become offended. This is one of several examples where we become victims to the vocal minority.

The minority amount of any group has a right to express their beliefs and opinions, but why do they have to share it outside their tribe? Why do normal people have to decipher their hidden agendas and listen to their monosyllabic diatribes?

Our most beloved freedoms, especially the freedom of speech is paramount for our existence. Unfortunately, it comes with a price. We had to listen to Sally Field's gobbledygook after she won her 2007 Emmy. However, most of us got lucky and only heard her whiny pitched voice ending with, "If the mothers ruled the world" before she was cut-off like a drunk. If the mothers ruled the world, we wouldn't have any children to carry on, so what was she trying to say? I should not have to listen to some invective diatribe from a celebrity. I wonder how many wars her sons endured. Naturally, somebody had to cry censorship the following day.

This was not an example of censorship. This was merely a moment in the spotlight for Sally to thank those for her award and get off the stage. Citizens watch the Emmys to see who is going to win an award, not listen to Sally's rant. This was not the right place or time for her to spew her opinion about the war in Iraq or her views about war. Does anybody think Sally can answer a double-jeopardy question correctly if the topic was about war? Sally, what year was the Battle of Hastings? I rest my case.

According to one poll taken shortly afterwards, only 37% of the respondents care what celebrities think about societal issues in general, yet another poll (Los Angeles Times) indicated that 80% of its respondents indicated it was a form of censorship by FOX Television. We all know how liberal The Los Angeles Times is, so I wonder how many times their employees voted. I want to hear Sally espouse her same ideology at a VFW on Memorial Day and not when she is at the Shrine Auditorium. Well, the Shrine Auditorium is not in the nicest place in the world, because it is located in an area of Los Angeles where you need bodyguards for your bodyguards.

Common sense should dictate our privilege of freedom of speech. Flag burning is infrequent, because the twerps with their Bics finally realized there is no free dentistry, yet it remains an impassioned topic. The US flag symbolizes everything we stand for, including freedom of speech, so why burn it. In 2006, the House of Representatives passed the Flag Protection Act that would become an amendment to our Constitution. This would allow each state to write their own laws and punishments for burning or desecrating the US flag. This would overturn the US Supreme Court's decision in 1989 in which it heard Texas v Johnson. On the other hand, it never passed in the senate. Thirty-four senators voted no, including Barbara Boxer, Joseph Lieberman, Joseph Biden, Barack Obama, Ted Kennedy, John Kerry, and Hillary Clinton, or simply known better as *the usual suspects*.

We have never had complete freedom of speech, nor should we. Legally, we should not commit libel, slander, perjury, or make certain verbal threats. You will not go to jail for making a racial slur, but I would not want to be the poor sap who calls Mike Tyson the N-Word or makes fun of his lisp. Mike's decorative swirl on his face, along with his mug shots, is funny enough. However, if I ever meet you Mike, my twin evil brother wrote this portion of the book. It is always better to think twice before you punch somebody outside the ring.

If it were a criminal offense to make a racial slur, then Michael Richards and Dog Chapman would be in a cell. The sight of Dog Chapman crying on national TV was priceless, yet watching Michael Richards on Youtube.com was pitiful at best. It is bad enough when the audience walks out on your routine, but now Michael ruined any chance for himself to star in Harlem Nights, part II.

Jesse Jackson and Al Sharpton - Racial Divide or Dumb and Dumber?

Michael Richards immediately apologized to Jesse Jackson after his debacle and Jesse accepted his apology, but Jesse does not speak for all people. Although he offered his services for the alleged rape victim at Duke University in 2006, he should have traveled one state south while he was there. He could have tackled the alleged sexual abuses at the Citadel, as reported by the school.

Prior to the Duke incident, Jesse referred to Jews as Hymies and New York City as Hymietown in 1984. I am glad he raised that point, because I was shocked at how many Jews I saw in the audience when I was performing at the Apollo theatre. After my performance, I repeatedly said, "Rav todot", but the audience merely stared at me. It was not until I shouted, "Peace" that I received my usual standing ovation. Oh, and the amount of Jews in Harlem is simply staggering. I never said shalom more times in my life. The folks in Harlem were kind, polite and openly wept as they told me, "Hitgaagati eleykha."

After that brilliant remark, which at first he denied, he then went on to say that Nixon's top advisors were German Jews. So, what is your point Jesse? My grandmother is Jewish. If you are tired of hearing the word Holocaust, we are even, because, I am tired of hearing about slavery and oppression. Do we have a deal?

According to an AP-AOL *Black Voices Poll* in 2006, Jesse received 15% of the votes as the most important black leader. Well, that translates to the fact that 85% of the people who took the poll did not feel that way. I think Grady from Sanford and Son would have garnered more votes.

Jesse- If you care to respond by radio, make sure your microphone is off-air. I would hate it if you called me white trash or any other disparaging remark behind my back. Be careful next time, because those microphones are touchy instruments. Unbelievably, something similar happened to me, but I dodged the bullet.

After a recent interview about my newly acquired island, I told a joke that was insensitive to poor people. I thought the interview was over when the reporter asked, "Why did you really buy a 50-acre island in the tropics?" I replied by stating the obvious, "Because I can." She uttered a sarcastic remark when I decided to retaliate by saying, "Yo Mama's so poor, she waves a Popsicle stick around and calls it air conditioning."

The following morning, I told the press that what I said was, "If your Mama and Papa are sick, I will make sure they have air conditioning." It only cost me a few thousand, but the positive press I received was immeasurable.

Eventually, we need to get together and trade Yo Mama jokes. Who doesn't like those silly and juvenile jokes? The only people that do not laugh are the hearing-impaired.

If you beat me, I will donate to your charity and if I win, you have to caddy for me at Augusta the next time I play. Regardless of who wins, this will demonstrate that blacks and whites can have fun, crack on each other's Moms and you would not know a 9-iron from an eggplant.

Al Sharpton annoys me like warm beer. As we all recall, he did not fair too well on the Tawana Brawley case in 1987. In 1991, shortly after the Crown Heights Riots, I do not think he did himself a favor by referring to Jews as diamond merchants. He allegedly said, "If the Jews want to get it on, tell them to pin their yarmulkes back and come over to my house." Oh Al, you really scare me. If I showed up at your house, you would crap in your pants and curl up in the fetal position. (Do not get your thong in a wad, because that was not a threat) Oh sweet Jesus! I need to take a break. I now have a vision of Al in a thong.

In 1995, he expressed his regrets by calling a Jewish tenant at Freddie's Fashion Mart a white interloper. I was actually shocked to hear Al use a four-syllable word. People can change their vocabulary, but they can never change their true character. I will ask my readers if Al fuels the flames in our racial divide. Sorry Al, they already answered yes.

In 2001, Al trespassed on US military territory. This little incident took place in Vieques, Puerto Rico. While spending his 90 days in jail, he decided to fast. I would not fast for anybody, even if I had his gut. However, we need somebody to help the illegal Mexicans who pick produce all day for below minimum wage. Can anybody imagine what Al's coif would look like after working in a lettuce field all day? I think it would look like a Jheri Curl, complete with activator.

In 2007, Al spoke to Don Imus on his radio show regarding Don's comments made on his radio show about the Rutgers women's basketball team. Al told Don, "Nappy is racial." Don replied, "Yes Sir. That is true."

I believe *diamond merchant* and *white interloper* fall into the racial index, so does that make Al a hypocrite or just plain stupid? At this very moment, I am receiving a response from my audience via my telepathic prowess. Sorry Mr. Sharpton, but my audience thinks you are a hypocrite and stupid. Wait, I am receiving more signals. Wow, they are also sending me signals that you are pathetic, lonely and dumb. I apologize Al, but I need to put on my earphones so I do not hear any more of this outlandish rubbish.

On January 4, 2008, Golf Channel broadcaster Kelly Tilghman and Nick Faldo were discussing how to stop Tiger Woods. Kelly said, "Lynch him in the back alley" and giggled. Al Sharpton's goal was to have her fired. Although the Golf Channel suspended her for two weeks, Al thought that was not good enough. Tiger Woods stated that Kelly and he are friends and the remark did not offend him. He considered this an open and shut case.

However, Al claims this is not about Tiger and it is about the civil injustice directed towards all African Americans, blah, blah, blah. Kelley did not commit a transgression Al! Tiger admitted his transgressions, albeit it pertained to a different story. I thought the only tiger that did something appalling in my lifetime was the one who almost ripped Roy's face off during his magic show.

In 2009, Al gave a eulogy at Michael Jackson's memorial and said, "Wasn't nothing strange about your Daddy. It was strange what your Daddy had to deal with. But he dealt with it anyway." Al, were you talking about the same Michael Jackson I know? The guy who made the Thriller album, right? You do not think he was strange. Hmm, the guy who wore one glove, slept with kids, had a house called Neverland and dressed like Captain Crunch? I think he was strange. It is always better to call a spade a spade, because beating around the bush has a completely different connnotation.

Kelly Tilghman-You are the reason I watch golf. I do not want to watch a bunch of men swinging around a metal rod. I want to see a cute commentator. Can you do me a favor sweetie? Can you and Natalie Gulbis give me golf lessons? I promise to behave, but I need to brush up on a few tricks I used to know. This will really embarrass Jesse when he hauls around my clubs at Augusta. Please email me at my usual address, but change your screen name to HOTGOLFCHICK, so my agent knows it is you. Tell Natalie she can use her normal screen name. Thanks a lot dolls and hopefully we will see each other soon.

Don Imus (The I-Man) - What can I say? You said it all on Sean Hannity's show on August 6, 2009. What a fantastic interview and I applaud you for your honesty. However, I never knew you to be anything less pertaining to the Rutgers comments. However, Al could not have made it a racial issue whatsoever, if you made fun of white basketball players.

I looked through hundreds of photographs of college and professional women's basketball teams wearing their uniforms and I came to this conclusion. The majority of black women that play basketball, whether for a college or professional team, look like a combination of Charles Barkley and Shaquille O'Neal. Conversely, the majority of white women that play basketball for a college or professional team, look like a combination of Larry Bird and Kevin McHale. (When they played)

Now that I am thinking about it, only Kelly Tilghman, Natalie Gulbis, chicks that play volleyball, about ten female tennis players, and a handful of gymnasts resemble women, in the sense they possess feminine qualities and sex appeal. There are also some hot-looking female surfers, but most female athletes look like lumberjacks.

PS Thanks for everything you do for kids with cancer at your ranch. Continued success, and God's speed with your health…..Sincerely….

Al Sharpton- I can actually picture you in the following scenario:

Shock Jock: *"Hey Al, this is Billy-Bob from KUTY in beautiful Palmdale."*

Sharpton: *"Palmdale! I hope you are not jiving me, because nobody has ever called me from the state of Greek. What can I do for you?"*

Shock Jock: *"Al, I tried to be funny today and said porch monkey on the radio."*

Sharpton: *"Do you olive eating, take-in-the-rear racists say porch monkey in Greek? That's appalling. I am flying to Greek tomorrow and I will arrange to speak with your elected officials regarding this irreprehensible language."*

Shock Jock: *"Al, I am in Palmdale, California and not* <u>Greece</u>. *I have done the honorable thing and fired myself. There is no reason for you to come here. I ended my career today, but I wanted to make you aware before the media storm hits."*

Sharpton: *"I will be there tomorrow."* Sharpton calls the local news station so they can tape Al's plane landing at Palmdale, CA.

Sharpton: After Sharpton exits the airplane, he finds the camera and says, *"I am here today to meet with Billy Bob from KUTY who said a disparaging and inflammatory remark against the African-American community."*

Sharpton: After locating the receptionist at KUTY says, *"Where is Billy Bob?"*

Receptionist: *"He wanted you to avoid leaving a huge carbon footprint in the air and that is why he called you yesterday and told you he fired himself."*

Sharpton: *A carbonated what?"*

Receptionist: *"Never-mind cupcake, but you have a nice day. By the way, who does your hair?"*

Al Sharpton, whether you like him or not, is one of the voices for civil injustices in the black community. Who is representing the Latino, Asian, and Indian races? Although Eskimos are also a race, there are not too many. Moreover, with the club-wielding expertise they possess, who would make a racial slur about them?

Al- Can you do me one favor please? The next time you get a haircut; would you send me a locket of hair? I do not know what I would do with it, but I am sure my cats would have fun with it. When my cats get tired of batting it around like a dead animal, I am sure I can use it to make a small whiskbroom.

If you need help from the white community, let me know. I have nothing to do, so the next time there is a march for an alleged racial incident, you buy and I will fly. Heck, can you imagine the two us getting drunk together? Oh brother- we would have a hoot! Just do not tell me anything I should not hear. Sometimes booze can cloud the judgment and all I want is a good laugh. Have your people contact my people. Thanks in advance for the invite.

Too many black entertainers use the N-word in their act. Although several prominent black leaders condemn the word, it has not stopped many comedians from continuing to abuse the word in their acts. I wonder if they substituted the N-word for *antique farm equipment*, would they still receive the same amount of laughs.

This is an example of freedom of speech. I think it is tasteless, but no matter how much our civilized country hates hearing this derogatory term, we must accept it. However, we all must remember equal rights under the law. If blacks use the N-word, there should be no discipline or retribution by advertisers, the media or anybody else if a white person chooses to use that worthless word. Races, cultures, and ethnicities do not own words.

As an example, I am not excusing Michael Richard's rant in any manner, because his inability to handle a heckler makes him a weak comic at best. As I understand it, this was the chain of events. They admitted approximately twenty people about halfway through his act. They were loud because many of them were ordering drinks. Apparently, this upset Richards and he yelled something. One of the people in the group said, "My friend doesn't think you're funny", which triggered the infamous rant. If I were Richards, I would have handled it like this:

Heckler: *"My friend doesn't think you're funny."*
Richards: *Did you say your boyfriend does not think I am funny?*
Heckler: *"I said my friend idiot."*
Richards: *"I'm sorry, I couldn't quite understand you. I don't know if you are retarded or have a speech impediment. Which one of you two*

lovebirds dresses as the cop from the Village People when you're feeling romantic? If you're not his boyfriend, then you must have just finished a mayonnaise sandwich.

This surely would have caused some people to laugh, however if the hecklers continued, it may have sounded like this:

Heckler and friend: *You suck Richards. What's a matter, can't find a job!*

Richards: *Your mama's lips suck too, but I don't bother her when she's doing her job. By the way, I am working right now. Do I interrupt your work? When you are emptying my trash, do I run outside and tell you to be gentle with my trashcans and make a big deal out of it in front of the neighbors? I can do this all night long. Hurry up and order so I can continue. By the way, they do not sell beer here in 40-oz bottles. You should have picked up a bottle from Pookie's Bar and Ribs around the corner.*

Michael Richards apologized for his rant on the David Letterman show via satellite. He referred to blacks as Afro-Americans during his apology, which is a term that went out in the 1970's. Damn Michael, when was the last time have you seen an Afro? His apology appeared insincere to me, as well as many people. However, I was not the dummy that went on a rant. I personally do not care if he ever gets another gig.

Listed below are comments from the last two decades that sparked controversy and a fervor between our continued racial divide and challenges to our first amendment rights. I wish it would simply go away, but I do not see it happening in my lifetime. The culprits behind the racial divide are the media, inbred parents and people who will not let well enough alone.

There are enough grown adults in the country who can distinguish the difference between a bad joke, slip of the tongue and a blatant racial comment. If people have to apologize for everything they say that might offend an individual or group, one would hear, *I am sorry* more often than Michael Moore's mirror. Sometimes, as in Michael Richard's case, I believe he fired himself, yet we do not need mouthpieces from either side guiding or misleading us in one direction or another. Here are some of the racial comments that made the highlight reel and I will let the reader decide if they should make the good, bad or tasteless list!

Racial slurs or was it a slow day in the news?

In 1997, PGA great Fuzzy Zoeller tried to be funny when he told reporters at the1997 Masters Tournament referring to Tiger Woods, "You pat him on the back and say congratulations and enjoy it and tell him not to serve fried chicken next year." Zoeller then smiled and quipped, "Or collard greens or whatever the hell they serve." I do believe that black people eat fried chicken and collard greens, just as I do. In fact, how many people in the South eat that same fare?

Tiger woods admitted the statement was funny and accepted an apology by Fuzzy. Unfortunately, K-Mart and Dunlop dropped him like a bad habit from their sponsorship roster. Gee, I wonder if K-Mart has ever had any racial discrimination lawsuits against them. Maybe somebody should look that up. I do not think his comments were racist in nature at all! Fuzzy is still the jokester on his tour and people should accept others for who they are. Now if this comment came from Vijay Singh, I would have been a little startled.

Howard Cosell, the legendary sportscaster, took too much heat from ABC, despite the fact he called Mike Adamle, a white football player a little monkey eleven years prior to his *little monkey* comment in 1983 against Alvin Garrett. I can hear the ABC brass back then huddled in their little office after that debacle:

"Down goes Cosell!"
"Down goes Cosel!"
"Down goes Cosell!"

Knowing that Cosell used this same name to describe a white person, I do not think he should have lost his job.

In 1988, Jimmy the Greek said, "The black is a better athlete to begin with because he's been bred to be that way—because of his high thighs and big thighs that goes up into his back, and they can jump higher and run faster because of their bigger thighs. This goes back all the way to the civil war when during the slave trading, the owner—the slave owner would breed his big black to his big woman so that he could have a big black kid." Holy crap, how many martinis did he have in order to scrounge up that diatribe?

Jimmy the Greek was canned, but deservingly so, in my opinion. When did he receive his PhD in genetics? Drinking and talking can be hazardous and if you do not believe me, ask Mel Gibson.

In the year 1999, Senator John McCain referred to his enemies as *Gooks*. Good job John! I have several friends and family members who are Vietnam Vets and they all refer to the Vietnamese as Gooks. The Honorable Senator has every right to call his captors Gooks. He was one of the bravest men in modern history, because how many other people can possibly withstand the daily physical and emotional pain he endured for over five years.

John did not coin the word and from my perspective, I do not expect any Vietnam Vet to call them anything less. It was a nasty and vicious war. Nevertheless, I have always wondered what the great senator would call Jane Fonda face-to-face and off-air. Some reporter wants to grill McCain about his choice of words in 1999, but somehow everybody has managed to forgive Hanoi Jane except the vets, and for good reasons.

Luckily, I did not have to go to Vietnam because I was only fifteen when the war ended. However, I always pay tribute to those men, as well as any man or woman who defends my rights. My dog in the fight is my country and I will defend veterans' honors as opposed to spitting on them when they return home from foreign soil as several anti-war activists did when our Vietnam Vets returned from war.

Therefore, if I understand the direction of our country, the far-left's ideology is supporting several groups whom are trying to pass *hate words* into state legislation, which would deem certain words illegal to say. That is censorship and violates every aspect of our Freedom of Speech. Yet, I bet it would still be permissible to spit on our troops as they arrive back from Iraq in case our anti-war zealots go bonkers again as they treated our Vietnam vets when they came home. My answer to their wishes is to buzz-off, because they will not win. I salute you Senator McCain and you received my vote! I apologize for the dummies that did not get it right.

In the year 2000, President Bush referred to Pakistanis as *Pakis*. This is considered a racial slur by several countries, especially Great Britain. Yet, the President as well as members of his staff were unaware this was an ethnic bomb. Although President Bush can appear to be dim-witted at times, he could have done a lot worse. He could have called them pak-men. I think the Pakistanis are far too sensitive. Besides, look at how many dot-heads answer the support calls for Dell Computers. Oops, is that India or Pakistan? I always get them confused, my bad if I got it wrong.

In 2003, Bill O'Reilly, host of the O'Reilly Factor, used the term *wetback*. I think he used it in the proper context when he was discussing the term coyote and wetback. The term coyote is somebody who smuggles Mexicans illegally across the border. In addition, I do not care how good of a swimmer somebody is, but if anybody swims the Rio Grande with or without a shirt, they are coming ashore with water on their backs. Mexicans born in this country, or entered our country legally, are not wetbacks. Moreover, I find this term offensive for the millions of Mexicans living in our country legally. The term wetback has been around a long time and that is how Mexicans received that nickname.

As far as Bill O'Reilly's alleged remarks in 2003, as cited by the Washington Post that accused Bill of saying, "I hope they're not in the parking lot stealing our hubcaps" referring to black people, I find incredulous. Bill was at a fundraiser for inner-city schoolchildren. Too many people wrote about this, but I cannot find a name of who supposedly heard Bill say it. Yet, I find it interesting there are several independent sites that continue to report this story. The scarier part about this is that Media Matters employ some of these individuals. Moreover, if Bill said something to the affect that Muslim women are ugly, as also alleged, I agree. Some have more facial hair than Chewbacca.

I do not know if the Cincinnati Police three-strike rule is still in effect, but in 2003, the Cincinnati police department granted their personnel three racial slurs before losing their job. The policy at the time cited the first two racial slurs would result in a suspension after each offense. If I were in a Cincinnati police station, I could envision the following conversation:

Officer Deepak: *Hey Serge, I have a question about our new policy.*

Sergeant: *Sure, what is it dot-head?*

Officer Deepak: *"Suppose I arrest an Irishman and say, I just arrested a potato-eating, clover-picking Leprechaun. Does that count as one or three strikes?"*

Sergeant: *Hey, cow-kisser, can't you count?*

Officer Deepak: *Well, I don't think potato eating is a racial slur, but the other two and paddy are one.*

Sergeant: *Well, bipty, that's a good question.* (Bipty is the enunciation for fifty and commonly heard at 7-11's) As an example, you may hear, *"the potato chips cost bipty cents."*

Captain: *"You are both fired!"*

In October of 2004, radio host Mark Belling also used the word wetback. The host from the Milwaukee radio station WISN said, "You're going to see every wetback and every other non-citizen out there voting." I cannot talk about his exact intent or subject matter, but the bottom-line is that Mark grouped non-citizens and wetbacks together. Wetbacks and non-citizens cannot vote, because they are here illegally. I don't see the big ado about this one either. Once again, certain far-left groups are popping up their heads starting to beat the tom-tom and chant the words *hate speech*. If a Mexican swims the Rio Grande and is in the US illegally, then he or she is a wetback. Have we become so sensitive, that we should start referring to them as Mark Spitz Wannabes? If they run across the border, do we call them athletes?

Legendary football coach Bill Parcells did not lose his job after he used the word *Jap* in 2004. After he made that remark, John

Tateishi said, "He sorely needs more education on what is offensive and non-offensive to Japanese-Americans." Where does someone receive educational assistance on what is offensive to the Asian culture? Is there a class to attend? I have confidence that Al Sharpton could handle those racial slurs as well. Can you imagine a conversation such as the following?

Parcells: *"Reverend, I apologize profusely for using the word Jap."*

Sharpton: *"You must understand the conflict and struggles the Japanese-Americans have gone though. Your remarks were way out of line."*

Parcells: *"I am ignorant of what is offensive and the Orientals bombed us first. What name is acceptable to call them besides Japanese-Americans? Perhaps they want to be called Americans."*

Sharpton: After some careful deliberation says, *"Pancake-face should work. Pancakes are an America food and this would help unify the two races with peace and harmony."*

In March of 2006, Dave Lenihan, who was a brand new talk host for KTRS said this when talking about Condoleezza Rice, "She loves football. She is African-American, which would kind of be a big coon. Oh my God, I am totally, totally, totally, totally sorry for that." Yeah and you should be Dave. Twenty minutes later, station president Tim Dorsey went on the air to announce that Lenihan was whacked. He made a slip of the tongue, because he meant to say coup, but how do you confuse those two words? Hey, at least he made Wikipedia and Condoleezza accepted his apology.

In July of 2006, Senator Joseph Biden said, "In Delaware, the largest growth of population is Indian Americans, moving from India. You cannot go into a 7-11 or a Dunkin' Donuts unless you have a slight Indian accent. I'm not joking." Well, in the 2000 Census, Delaware reported 16,000 out of 783,000 people said they were from another race. Whites accounted for 585,000 and blacks accounted for 150,000. Gee, where are all the Indians? Joseph must have seen a million Indians move into his state in the last few years.

I thought his comment was funny, because no matter what 7-11 I enter, there appears to be one in every establishment. I know what he was saying and I do not agree this is a racial slur, but an astute observation.

In fact, in July of 2007, 7-11 turned twelve of their locations into Kwik-E-Marts in helping to promote The Simpsons Movie. I particularly do not watch the show, but I know there is an Indian who is running the store in the weekly cartoon. Thank you, Come Again! Sadly, Joseph Biden is now our Vice President.

In May 2006, former white house speaker, Tony Snow, said "tar baby" Oh My God, somebody get Al Sharpton to take care of this fiasco. Tony used tar baby to indicate a sticky situation. End of story people, move it along, nothing to see here. It was not a racial slur as some people labeled it. This never should have been a newsworthy story.

In May 2006, Mitt Romney, the man who will not be president, said the same word as Tony Snow. He too was referring to a *sticky situation*. John Amato wrote, "What is wrong with these people?" My question to Mr. Amato is what is your problem? Do you have any real journalistic work to perform? Move it along, nothing to see here either.

In the latter part of January of 2007, Joseph Biden said the following, "Obama is the first mainstream African-American who is articulate and bright and clean." If Biden added the words, presidential candidate after African American, it would have mitigated his stupidity. Jackson and Sharpton ran for president, but I think neither one is articulate. Colin Powell would have fit the bill entirely and so would Condoleezza Rice. In fact, there are several more. Tavis Smiley is one of thousands of bright and articulate black men, but sadly, he did not run for president.

In March of 2007, while speaking at the Conservative Political Action Convention, Anne Coulter, the blonde and leggy conservative columnist and author said, "I was going to have a few comments about the other Democratic nominee, John Edwards, but it turns out that you have to go into rehab if you use the word faggot." I thought it was a very funny line. She was making a comparison to Isaiah Washington who used the same term, according to T.R. Knight, and allegedly attended anger management classes. We also know that John Edwards is not gay. It was in jest, yet she used the most derogatory term in the gay community.

If I were Anne Coulter, my choice of words for the same meaning would have been *shirt-lifter* or *backstabber* because they are a lot funnier. Besides, she probably could have left the convention before the crowd understood her innuendo. Not to get too far off track, but do we have to attend anger management classes if we say *fart knocker* or *rump ranger?* I just want to know my rights in case I slip.

In June 2007, Brit Hume called John Glenn a "*partisan-spear chucker*". I think Brit has been at his job for too long. He has those droopy eyes akin to a sad looking beagle, and perhaps he just lost it; I do not know. Nevertheless, what was he thinking? It could not have been construed as a racial remark, because the last I checked; Sen. John Glenn is still white. I do not even know what he was trying to say, but I do not think he did either. Bad boy Brit, now go outside and lay down. You are rather lucky that you were not talking about Colin Powell.

In October 2007, a character on TV received attention for making a supposed racial slur. Teri Hatcher's character on Desperate Housewives said, "Can I check those diplomas because I want to make sure they're not from some med-school in the Philippines" during a medical examination. My initial reaction, as well as my reaction now is who cares. There were some irate viewers, who wrote ABC, and they spun the story like a top and the rest is history. I thought it was a funny line.

The majority of my friends overwhelmingly voice their opinions about doctors from foreign countries. I do not want anybody operating on me if he sounds like a computer manufacturer's customer service representative. I am rather fussy, but if I am bleeding to death, I do not care who it is, just help me. I have had bad experiences from American and foreign doctors, yet I prefer to converse with one that I can fully understand. It is hard enough to understand Latin and medical terms from a Yankee, but it makes me want to cry when I hear those same terms from somebody who has a hard time enunciating the word fifty.

Next in line for a slip of the tongue was Andy Rooney. In August of 2007, Andy wrote, "....but today's baseball stars are all guys named Rodriguez to me. They're apparently very good but they haven't caught my interest." Why would anybody with an average brain raise this as an issue? Andy was wrong for saying what he did, because there are only twenty-three men named Rodriguez and twenty-six named Hernandez. Did Andy really make a racial slur? Not in my opinion, because he also overlooked the seventeen men named Ramirez who play baseball. Andy is in his eighties and from his perspective; he was clearly in the right to make that assertion. The names in baseball have changed over the course of his life and that is the story. This should not have made the press and shame on those who tried to whip this story into anything else.

Anne Coulter did it again in October of 2007. Anne said the old *camel jockey* slur, but she defended herself eloquently and passionately. On the October 1 edition of Hannity and Colmes, Anne Coulter told Hannity and Colmes the term *camel jockey* was in her book, aptly titled, *If Democrats had any brains, they'd be Republicans*. Well, do not worry about it Anne, because they do not have any brains, therefore I do not want them on my team.

Putting politics aside for one minute, Anne's defense for saying *camel jockey* is the fact that Arabs killed 3,000 Americans when they flew the planes into New York's twin towers. Anne showed no remorse by her comment and further added, "We have sure moved away from the day when we called them Krauts and Nips."

I could not agree with her more. My uncle served for 40 years in the US Navy. He saw action in WWII, Korea and Vietnam. Krauts, Nips and Gooks are terms of endearment to him. As I stated earlier, just because I did not tote a gun around during times of our armed conflicts, yet my country is in the fight; therefore I will always respect the speech of our soldiers.

If my Uncle, or any other veteran, is a racist because they use words such as those, the people who choose to label them a racist are mere cowards. I respect Anne's position for not backing down. In her particular case, she is right. Arabs attacked this country, therefore if she chooses to call them camel-jockeys, then so be it. I refer to them as *carpet pilots* at times, so what is the big deal? At least I do not call them *checkpoints*.

What do you think our soldiers called the enemy in this present war, or even Desert Storm? In order to dehumanize the enemy, one of the objectives is for the enemy to have a name. Our soldiers heard rag-head, towel-head, etc. before they saw actual combat. The labeling of our enemies during time of war is for psychological reasons and it has several effective uses. Therefore, does it make all of our soldiers racists if they use those types of slurs? I passionately argue no.

Anne- Don't forget to write me back. I changed my email address again due to the constant harassment from the paparazzi. My old email address no.slak@yahoo.com is temporarily shutdown. Please use studmuffinsmartman@Iwantubabe.com. Thanks.

In November 2007, Carla Dartez, a democratic state representative from Louisiana said, "Talk to you later Buckwheat", as she was ending a phone conversation with the mother of the local NAACP president. Carla is a white democrat and this thing never went anywhere, until it came time to vote shortly thereafter. However, the good news is that she lost her race to a republican. Talk to you later, loser!

On January 9, 2008 Chris Mathews from MSNBC alluded that Hillary Clinton would not be affective in winning her Senator seat and perhaps her current position as a presidential contender if it were not for her husband's philandering ways. He took a lot of crap from Media Matters and women's groups; including The View, a show that makes me queasy. Chris apologized later on-air for his opinion, but there is some truth to his comments in my opinion as well. For those of you with short-term memory loss, look at Hillary's past.

Hillary was in complete denial for one solid year regarding Monica Lewinsky. She went on the Today Show in 1998 and mumbled something about a right-wing conspiracy theory to Matt Lauer. She spent a lot of time defending her husband on and off camera. The point is moot. Bill is an admitted philander and liar. If Hillary wants to put up with him, that's her business. However, I also think it is responsible journalism to raise these issues.

Would it have been rude if Chris Mathews resurfaced Whitewater, Travel-gate, Clinton v. Jones, as well as any other scandal during the Clinton administration? The answer is a resounding no. I think putting the Clintons back in the White House is like giving Siegfried and Roy the same tiger. Furthermore, how many times do I have to hear the words misogyny or misogynistic coming from these women groups? If Chris Mathews reads Playboy, does that make him misogynistic or a man who knows what he likes?

In February 2008, David Shuster from MSNBC said the Clinton campaign had *pimped out* the Clintons' daughter on live TV. I think it was a terribly funny line, but he had to apologize. The usual suspects, including Media Matters, pounced on this story like a fat person on a cheeseburger. In the literal sense of the phrase, I doubt if she could make any money as a prostitute. However, the phrase *pimped out* is part of our American slang. It's kind of like saying, "I think Hillary is *pimping herself out* every time she cries." I'm just glad that David Shuster did not say that about Obama's wife. Al Sharpton probably would have jumped on that story like a fat woman on a sorbet.

On July 28, 2009, Glenn Beck told his friends at FOX *he believes* Obama is a racist. Glenn is entitled to his opinion, because this is freedom of speech. I bet his advertisers sharted in their pants when they heard this remark.

Yet, it is ironic that one of Obama's czars mysteriously quit after America heard him making racial remarks. Van Jones, the Green Jobs czar, quit on September 6, after videos showed him making blatant racial remarks. At least it's a safe assumption he would never receive a thumbs-up for the White Jobs czar in the near future.

This was after Glenn stated his opinion. There is more information coming out on other people in the administration also making racial slurs about white people. Maybe Glenn is right. I do applaud the fact Glenn is not afraid to say what he wants. As long as he maintains his ratings, he won't go anywhere, nor should he.

Moreover, I find it interesting why Al Sharpton or Jesse Jackson did not jump on his statement. I think they both knew they would have lost, not to mention that Obama had already erred by referencing an alleged racial profiling that led to the infamous beer summit on July 30.

I do not like President Obama or Clinton. I would not call either of them a racist. I would have no problem in calling them stupid and arrogant, but not racists. If I could ask Glenn Beck one question, it would be the following:

Dear Mr. Beck- Do you ever have a craving for Ritalin? If I could ask one more question sir…would you mind asking Gretchen Carlson to send me an autographed photo?

Without any reservation, she has the best-looking legs in the media. The Internet is proud to show those sticks-- yippee! However, nothing says it better than an autographed photo.

Gretchen, if Glenn does not give you the message, email me later tonight. Use my *Dreamboat* account, so we can keep this quiet. I always wanted to know if you were Swedish. If you are, then you have good genes and probably look good in them too. We will talk later Gretchen.

At least we do not have to worry about Steve or Brian making any remarks that could be construed as racial. However, it appears that Steve stares at Gretchen's legs more often than Brian does. I find that odd, since he is married. I could be wrong, but that is my observation.

There are literally thousands of different ethic terms, jokes and stereotypes. There are jokes about the Polish, Italians, White, Blacks, Jews and everything in between. I did not know that *925* was a racial slur towards blacks. That number signifies a *suspicious person* in L.A. Police jargon. While also researching for this book, I discovered that the term *slurpee-jockey* is a racial slur towards Indians. A *shipwrecked Mexican* is a racial slur towards Puerto Ricans. The list of supposed racial slurs is endless. So, when does it end? If new ones pop-up everyday, then how do we stop it?

I find nothing funny whatsoever about the N-Word, but even my black friends laughed at *925*. Everybody says stupid things all day long and I am not condoning the egregious racial slurs, but people should take them for what they are worth. Simply, consider the source.

Paris Hilton has not only been heard making racial slurs, but she is one. Unbelievably, a Paris Hilton is a racial slur. The definition of a Paris Hilton is a white person who represents everything negative in the stereotypical WASP woman. This pinhead isn't even thirty, but has now managed to make it onto a racial slur Internet site? Nice move cupcake…..

Jeff Foxworthy is a very funny comedian, but the racial slur *redneck* does not offend me. I think he has the best routine in the business. Yet, would he be as funny if he referred to his audience as crackers, wiggers, or white trash?

The point I am asserting is that we are all going to say stupid things that annoy or hurt an individual of another race. We have become too sensitive to what we hear, as opposed to its intent. It is my opinion that most so-called racial slurs are an ill-fated attempt at comedy, or a form thereof. There are deliberate and pointless attacks against all races and those are the ones I find offensive. However, let our Freedom of Speech prevail, because the chronic offender of blatant racial remarks will eventually self-destruct.

It should not be the job of a handful of people to tell us what is right or wrong to say, because normally it is coming from their perspective only. As I stated earlier, there are tort laws to remedy some situations, as well as federal laws protecting all races from harassment in the workplace. We would only divide the racial boundaries if we continue to dissect every comment or statement that any particular race thinks is racial.

I think the media is as much to blame as anybody else. If an alleged racial slur hits the airwaves, do we need to continue to beat it like a rug? That is merely fanning the flames of an out of control fire. The comment about Tiger Woods by Kelly Tilghman is a great example. Tiger responded by saying, "Were friends; no big deal." It is at that point, the media should drop it, along with everybody else.

Tiger Woods will continue to be the best golfer in the world, unless he has to play another little Asian feller for the PGA championship. Y.E. Yang just beat Tiger like a rented mule for the 2009 PGA Championship. Y.E. Yang is now the wealthiest person in Seoul, Korea, excluding Samsung.

Tiger will never win husband of the year award, but that's his problem. He is still a great golfer, but that's not a prerequisite to get into heaven. I'd rather have a crappy round of gold than embarrass myself and family to the world. I will never have to use the word transgression in my life. I don't want to belabor the point, but that had to be damn embarrassing, huh? Tiger is probably sweating like Mike Tyson at a spelling bee.

Don't forget to call me Tiger if your game gets rusty, I'll give you some lessons.

Television can make you stupider!

Shows produced for television are also a form a freedom of speech, despite having the FCC. Most of today's shows on television are rubbish. It doesn't matter where I go, I have to hear what recently happened on American Idol, Dancing with the Stars, Extreme Home Makeover, The Bachelor, The Biggest Loser, along with an assortment of other trashy TV shows. If it were not for the History and Discovery channel, I would have thrown my TV through the wall. Maybe our Diversity Czar Mark Lloyd, can do something about this egregious amount of trash on TV. Here's my opinion on the following shows:

American Idol- It looks like the days of Paula Abdul appearing under the influence of a heavy dose of barbiturates on this show ended. I didn't know if she had a speech impediment or just simply drowsy all the time. It is bad enough when Randy Jackson critiques the contestant. We all know how many best-selling albums he made as lead vocalist. Yet, with all due respect, he should be able to hit the higher notes since his gastric bypass surgery.

Simon Cowell is merely mimicking Judge Judy or Anne Robinson. The concept of letting his stinging one-liners fly is refreshing, but nothing new. If one of the contestants can't carry a tune, Simon simply lets him or her know it in the most affective manner, bluntly. Paula Abdul appeared to like every young man, Randy looks like he is hungry; therefore, Simon is the one who brings any true talent to the show.

However, despite the ratings, the show simply lacks anything of substance. Ryan Seacrest is the Emcee of the show, but name a TV or radio show where you don't see his mug. His image is just as ubiquitous as a missing kid's face on a milk container. Ryan Seacrest gets more attention than an Amber alert. We never hear about the kid who won at the Special Olympics, but we always hear Ryan's name. Wow, how shallow are we?

The Bachelor- If American Idol is lacking in substance, this show is lacking in every other conceivable notion. I think this show managed to find the bottom of hell. It is a show for people with a thirst for ignorance. I bet Stevie Wonder doesn't watch this garbage. He may not see, but he can still hear, and who wants to hear a bunch of girls with teased-hair fighting over some fruitcake?

The concept of having approximately twenty girls fighting over one man doesn't happen in real life. How many girls fought over Rock Hudson or Clay Aiken? This only happens behind the stage of a rock concert or in my crib. This show merely proves the adage there are too many people who are desperately seeking attention. Hookers aren't seeking attention, they are seeking money. I think the girls on this show are seeking attention and money. Does that make them worse than a hooker? I think the answer was just given, but I'll let the reader decide.

The word bachelor means a man who is not or has never been married. One would think these thimble-headed twits vying for his affection might realize he has a problem, hence that is why he is still single. Some of the bachelors look like they could be on the cover of GQ, so why is he still single? If I were a single woman looking for Mr. Right, I would check any pedophile sites, his credit score and school grades before I started fighting with the other girls for his attention.

Hell's Kitchen- Cook Gordon Ramsay is merely an Anne Robinson with a blonde version of Ty Pennington's coif. I prefer the word cook, as opposed to the French version of the same profession, a chef. When do people know they have become a chef and are no longer a cook? I guess you become a chef when the overtime stops and you become salaried. Mr. Ramsay hurls insults at people who can't get it right the first time around. I can only imagine the first time he cooked bubbles and squeak, he didn't get it right either. If he yelled at me like one of his contestants, I would hit him in the head with the blunt end of his knife.

His sarcasm is priceless, and he's a lot quicker on his feet than his counter part Simon Cowell, but it's rare to find two witty people across the pond. If he does not lose his teeth, like most Brits, this show may actually last. It appeals to people who like to see cooks berated for not cooking shrimp properly. Who doesn't like that kind of television? It's funny, but it too is lacking in intellectual value.

Dancing with the Stars- Despite its ratings, I do not see how this show survives! This is a show where we get to see *stars* dancing with true dancers. Is ABC so desperate, they'll let anybody on the show? So far, they had a one-legged woman, George Hamilton, (Who I thought was dead) and Steve Wozniak. The producers should let Stevie Wonder have a chance at reinventing himself. As opposed to watching a prosthetic leg possibly fly into the audience, we could watch Stevie dance. I can assure you that he has a good chance of creating some new break dancing moves, whether they are intentional or not. Moreover, this show really proves that white people couldn't find rhythm in a song if they had one leg or two.

I was able to see Marie Osmond collapse and almost crack her coconut. That was the highlight from that year. I always look for the blonde professional dancer when she does the splits. I do not care if she does not know the difference between the Paso Doble and Viennese Waltz, her dances always come together after she does the splits. Critics who argue that the Tango is the most romantic dance in the world have obviously never watched her perform. I think most people watch the show to see who is going to fall, see who is attracted to each other, or watch in horror as a plastic leg knocks somebody out sitting in the front row.

Therefore, the 28th Amendment would slightly alter our first amendment rights. It would still allow people to say what they want, without consequences incited by the media. If I think Rosie O'Donnell looks like a fat hog, then I should have the right to say it without any consequences from the media or the sensitivity Gestapo.

Special Interest Groups
– Sweaty Citizens

The 28th Amendment would eradicate all SIGs like a wheat bug in Kansas. They are nothing more than a pity-party and a cog in the wheel of progress. We should stop catering to the vocal minority and stick to the original ideology and beliefs that helped form this country. It is ironic that a minority of individuals can make the majority's life a living hell. I thought only fleas, tics, and crabs could do such a thing.

Their lives became wretched, because they have nothing to do, which allows them plenty of free time. When you take a positive and turn it into a negative, it creates havoc and turmoil. There are literally hundreds of political advocacy groups, political action committees, pressure groups, etc. The one thing they have in common is a little *donate here* button on their websites.

These SIG's annoy me to the ends of the Earth. Most of them have a Draconian attitude, in the sense they are not bashful about ramming their twisted ideology down your gullet. In fact, because they are tax-exempt, I'm thinking about starting my own. I am going to start my own organization called PSTFU.org. The acronym says it all and I will raise funds to continue to stop any new ones from arising. Naturally, any contributors would have to value my opinion. Unlike several of them, I have no hidden agenda and I promise not to send any money to politicians, unless they like me. All contributions will help in keeping my website running.

There will always be jokes about gay people, fat people, different races, slow people, Ryan Seacrest, and different ethnicities, etc. We should all be tolerant of others to a certain degree, but it does not mean we have to accept their cause or beliefs. Somehow, I managed to land on the NAAFA site. This is the National Association to Advance Fat

Acceptance. Their mantra is "We come in all sizes….Understand it, support it and accept it." No, I don't have to accept anything if I don't want to and that's one of the problems that resonates from special interest groups. Fat people have the same rights as the rest of us! Fat, thin, bald or ugly, the constitution already protects all of us.

I guess I should premise my definition of fat. My definition of fat does not constitute a beer-belly on a man, or *junk in the trunk* on a woman. Unless, the junk amounts to the Sanford and Son collection, because that means somebody has a junkyard in their britches. I'm not referring to pleasantly plump or even to what some people refer to as midsize. I'm talking about super-sized plus! I'm talking about fat people so huge, that groceries scream for help when these people waddle down the aisle. That is my definition of fat.

If I choose not to tolerate fat people, it's my business. However, the NAFFA site made me curious. I found another site that mentioned we should stop referring to kids as obese. I do not call any kid obese unless he or she is fat enough to be qualified. Even then, I hardly ever use the word obese. I call fat little orbs the following names: Two-tons, super-sized, butterball, tub-o-lard, destroyer, wicker-crippler, etc. Everybody must understand that obesity does not breakout like leprosy; it takes time! If you have a plump little kid, put the blinders on him or her when you take them food shopping. Don't take them off until you're in the fruit and vegetable section and be sure to keep your little sphere out of the cookie and pasta aisles.

Some other fat sites, just like any other SIG, solicit for people wishing to volunteer. I wouldn't want to volunteer for any fat organization for fear of cannibalism. If one thing annoys me about fat people, it is their objection to pay for two seats on an airplane. Hey, I am trying to save the environment and it takes more fuel to burn to carry the extra weight. This does not include the irritation I receive when sitting between two huskies. I am referring to the irritation I get on both sides of my arms from the fat that is constantly rubbing up and down on them.

What about Jimmy Hoffa, does anybody think he is lost in any unnecessary folds of blubber? That poor Jimmy! He probably screamed for days and nobody heard him. He is probably wedged into a fold of fat containing a bucket of chicken and some ding-dongs. Is it a possibility he volunteered for a fat organization prior to his disappearance? By now, he probably looks like a cooked strip of bacon.

Here is a couple of interesting stories regarding fat people and I can't make this kind of stuff up. The medical examiner's offices of Orange and Osceola counties in Florida received new autopsy tables. They now support 1,000 pounds as opposed to the old ones that could handle 300 pounds. Yeah, and I have a good bet on how these rotund people succumbed. Surely, it was not from malnutrition.

In addition, the medical examiners are in need of drawers to store the bodies. I would take this approach. First, find out if they are in need of a crematorium. If so, store the body parts in the various bins and forget about it. Can you imagine the ashes of a 1,000-pound person dropped from an airplane into the sea at once? This could cause a tsunami of epic proportions. If anybody thinks that Lake Okeechobee does not have a measurable tide, drop ashes from a 1,000-lb person in that body of water and see what happens.

A more disturbing article also recently came out of Florida. This story came out of Stuart, Florida. Before I continue, is it something in the water or pork chops that is causing the people in Florida to balloon up so much? I have not felt this nauseous since I watched the last episode of The Biggest Loser.

A 4'-10" 480-pound woman was literally *stuck* to her couch. I mean stuck, as in dead-stuck. She apparently had been couch-ridden for six years. The emergency workers had to remove her doors to take her and the couch to the hospital. Her skin was *stuck* to the fabric of the couch. After towing her fabric-ridden carcass to the hospital, she died shortly thereafter.

I hope she did not have to pay for a hospital bed. I want to know who was looking after this woman. I guess cameras would not have done any good for monitoring purposes, because it may appear there would have been a never-ending period of darkness on the monitor.

Am I supposed to feel sorry for these types of people, I don't know. I grapple with mental anguishes like this as fat people grapple for fish or anything else that moves. It is tough, but at which point in one's life does it take them to get help. How many pounds does one have to gain before they realize they cannot move? They should pick up the phone and call for help. Perhaps they do, but it keeps slipping out of their hands from pork grease or they already ate it. The Eskimos can hear walruses from miles away, so why fat people do not scream for help is a mystery to me.

What would Dr. Phil tell these people besides, "Could you pass the biscuits and gravy please?" Everybody needs help, but the oldest line in the world is those who help themselves first to second servings gain weight quicker, or something similar. I wanted to be in denial when I wrote my first book when I wrote about this same subject. In fact, I thought the statistics were unfounded and were not right, well I digress. After writing about these two stories and visiting some other web sites dedicated to fat people, I am starting to believe that most Americans are overweight.

All I hear are stories about starving people in the world and then I read these atrocious stories of food abuse and it makes me wonder. I wonder how many ding-dongs, pork rinds and hotdogs these people ate to gain this kind of weight. I wonder if my taxes are going to help support these people, because at this very moment, I cannot think of anything else that could support them.

Where do these huskies shop? It dawned on me to perform my own investigation. If a person cannot leave their couch, then the food has to arrive to them. I went to Amazon.com and discovered my worst fears. They are advertising Kraft Macaroni & Cheese for sale. Now get a load of this crap, no pun intended. From Amazon, you can buy a 24-Pack of their 7.25oz boxes of Kraft Macaroni and Cheese. This is not your normal cheap variety; this is their three-cheese stuff! Amazon also advertises you can receive your shipment the next day!

Who buys 24 packs of mac & cheese? Oh my God, does the UPS dude have to blow his back out every time he delivers to one of these sweat hogs? I personally hate the looks and smell of this mac & cheese, but if I wanted to load up on some carbohydrates, I guess this makes sense. I tried to find hot-dogs on Amazon's site, but I was unsuccessful. Most of these spheres love to eat cut-up hotdogs in their heaping pile of melted butter, powdered-cheese and pasta. I'm getting queasy again, but it's all part of the job. I guess I'd rather be writing about this, than the poor sap who's writing obituaries for the upcoming edition of Fat and Grotesque Monthly.

How does someone begin to write an obituary for the morbidly obese that die in precarious manners without cracking up? I guess it would be easier than performing the eulogy at a funeral looking at a stiff in an open casket. Well, normal sized caskets would be open. An appropriate eulogy could be as follows:

Eulogist: *Dear friends and family members, we are gathered here today in close quarters to say goodbye to Bertha. She was a strong woman and she was a biggin' too. If her heart were as large as her body, there would be no wars or starving people in this world. She meant a lot to all of us, especially the UPS dude who is joining us today. He would like to say a few words. Please come up and comfort us with your gentle words of sorrow.*

UPS Dude: *For the past sixteen years, I delivered a 24-pack of mac and cheese to Bertha on a weekly basis. I struggled up three flights of stairs to her dusty apartment. After pushing the doorbell, I had to endure the hot sun baking my head as I patiently waited for Bertha to make the long and overbearing 25-foot walk to the door. After she let me in, I had to move the smelly pots, pans and empty boxes of mac and cheese, so I could gently place her new shipment on her kitchen counter. I am going to miss her like a bad rash and my new property taxes.*

Eulogist: *Is there anybody else who would like to say a few kind words?*

Amazon CEO: *I would!*

Eulogist: *Please, come on up.*

Amazon CEO: *Miss Bertha was one of our loyal customers. Because of her generous support, our stock is solid as a tank, just like her. Her unfortunate demise has left a generous surplus of our Kraft Macaroni and Cheese sold in the 24-pack. We are dropping our prices by 10% in her honor. If there is anybody here that would like to place an order, please be sure to see my assistant on your way out of the building.*

Eulogist: *Is there anybody else who would like to say a few kind......*

A sudden rush of fat people attending the wake, trample the UPS dude and CEO of Amazon into the ground, causing them to blend into the tile grout. Next, the runaway stampede inadvertently crushes the CEO's assistant. The stampede continues on their way through the brick wall in search of the once slender assistant. It is not until they realized what happened that they slow down.

The slow moving bovines continue to their vehicles with their chins held low in disbelief. They sadly entered their SUV's and minibuses to drive home. When one of the massive women started crying, her friend waddled over to comfort her. She stated it was not her fault, because all of them were responsible for the stampede. The weeping woman said she wasn't crying over the destruction and loss of life she caused, but she was crying because she noticed the red light was on at Krispy Kreme across the street and forgot her pocketbook.

Special Interest Groups
– Cigarette Nazis

I find any nonprofit group that spews their opinion about nonsmoking just as ridiculous, and there are plenty of them on the web. Who elected these groups as the crusaders against smokers? Has anybody been paying attention to these people? You can join their group, or other similar groups to get advice on how to jump on any class-action lawsuits against cigarette manufacturers. Well, good luck. Although I smoke like a broken chimney, I jumped on the Florida class-action suit. This was a good chance for receiving lots of money. I wanted to see if somebody would pay me for something I like to do.

I knew perfectly well, the majority of times jurors spew out ridiculous judgments when it comes to class-action lawsuits and sure enough, the thimble-headed Miami jurors awarded $145 billion in punitive damages in 2000. There were approximately 700,000 smokers at the time in Florida, thus allowing them $207,000 each. Instantly, the numbers ran though my mind faster than a cop yells, *"Quit resisting!"* during an episode of Cops. This would have provided me with enough money to purchase 8,280 cartons of cigarettes. I could have smoked two cartons a week for the next eighty years. My thought of moving into the Playboy Mansion was no longer my number one dream. I openly wept when the State Supreme Court overturned their judgment and stated smokers would have to file individual lawsuits in 2006.

I am at a disadvantage and cannot sue, because I would have to visit some land shark, or at least fill out some type of paperwork online. I cannot travel to a lawyer's office to file a complaint, because I wheeze when I drive, let alone walk to my car. Typing is just as hard, because I wheeze every time I hit the space bar on my keyboard. I don't know if it's in the timing, or my thumb is numb from holding the butt-end of a cigarette for twenty plus years. Regardless, I did not make the January 11 deadline to sue. So far, about 1,800 people are suing. Half of those people are dead and suing for wrongful death, well, they're not suing, but somebody is on their behalf. I guess it is hard to sue if you are all shriveled up and in the bone-yard. Did anybody preserve a charcoal-looking lung, or did people only bring a death certificate and a copy of the autopsy report? It's still a gamble trying to take on the cigarette companies, but even a blind squirrel can find a nut, even though most of the time they find the bottoms of moving car tires.

Here is my real gripe about any hard-core, non-smoking group. They have managed to lobby their way through all the red tape and made my life hell. Has anybody ever died from secondhand smoke? My answer is, prove it. Has anybody read an autopsy report that stated such findings? The answer is a resounding no. The secondhand smoke theory blossomed under a report by Sir George Godber in 1975. I had a problem when the medical community from the UK espoused his scientific findings.

The UK is a country that looks as though their citizens are using Chinese toothpaste, so the credibility within their scientific community is questionable at best. Eleven years later, comments by C. Everett Koop, our former Surgeon General virtually echoed Godber's report. Well, if secondhand smoke is harmful, I think I would see a rise in nonsmokers getting some form of heart decease. I could punch more holes in their reports than a donut maker punches donut holes. Words such as *can*, *suggest* and *expected* are meaningless in fact-finding reports. These words are resonating in Koop's report.

By 1990, airliners no longer allowed passengers to smoke. However, this slipped under the radar like a stealth bomber. Was this the work of another lobbying group, or from an unforeseen stewardess whining committee? Approximately fifteen years have passed and I would like to see a report on how many nonsmoking stewardesses got lung cancer or died from a direct result from secondhand smoke. By the looks of things, more stewardesses have a better chance of dying from obesity.

They managed to change the weight restrictions in the late seventies and early eighties. Read the lawsuit leveraged at United Airlines by stewardesses in 1992. Some sued for weight harassment and some sued for age discrimination. So, what's their point? I expect someone young enough to open the hatch door and someone who can sashay down the aisle without their hips rattling both chairs on the ends. Why do I need to scoot over when the liquor cart comes down the aisle? Why am I asked if I'm strong enough to open the emergency door? That's their job, not mine! Therefore, if I have to tolerate their nonsense, then I should smoke and look at a nice pair of legs walking down the aisle. I don't need a male stewardess named *Evan* asking me if I want a pillow.

In 1993, the Clampetts, better known as the Clintons, banned smoking after White House dinners, but Bill Clinton thought it was okay for an intern to smoke a pipe in the Oval Office. I guess it's politically correct to call it *advanced* massage therapy. Oh yeah, I think there was something about a cigar in the Oval office too. I guess cigars and pipes were okay in the Oval Office, but nobody could smoke a cigarette after a nice meal. Gee, at least President Regan let you smoke after his dinners. Moreover, in 1993, when Hillary banned smoking from the White House, the percentage of smokers in this country was 27%, as opposed to 40% in 1964. According to the American Heart Institute, 21% of Americans still smoke.

I smoke so much, I went ahead and painted my house walls that yellow-tar color, so when I move pictures, I don't have to repaint. In fact, everything in my house is the same color. My toilet, tub, walls, appliances all have that cigarette tar-color. My house smells worse than the El Cortez Casino in Las Vegas. My house smells like a heaping pile of cigarette butts, because I not only want to see where my money is going, I want to smell it too.

Why do people who smoke still want to sue? They just need to read the warnings on the sides of cigarette packages. I don't think there is a doctor in the western civilization that does not agree that cigarette smoking is bad for your health. Smokers should see the signs of their health deteriorating. I'm only 47, but I get dizzy when I get off the commode and I can't run near the distances I could when I was twenty. I can see the physical changes, as well as the brown tar I spit up occasionally. If I cough too long, I see those little asteroids floating around my eyes for about a half an hour. I'm in it for the endurance, because I'm not a quitter.

Some nonprofit groups on the Internet boasts where nonsmokers can get legal forms to help *protect their rights*. Did I miss something in the Constitution again? If they are citing the 14th amendment, then I can play that game too. Groups like these are aiding and helping to enact state laws by shoveling tons of money at various legislatures. (That's how it works) Yet, what about the part of "Nor shall any state deprive any person of life, liberty…." Where is my liberty to smoke? I guess that went up in smoke along with several other things, because organizations with enough money can get several stupid laws passed. Oh well, try to stop me from smoking in my house. I support and donate to our second amendment, not to some group that resembles the Special Olympics kids who want me to stop smoking.

I just returned home from the liquor store, and something caught my attention before I entered that joint. I noticed prior to entering the establishment, there were no public ash urns to discard the lit cigarette dangling from my bottom lip. It dawned on me that over the years, there are less ash urns in front of any establishment. Therefore, I did what anybody would do in my predicament. I flicked the freaking thing about six feet to the side of the entrance without looking.

It could have landed on top of a midget's head thus causing a burnt skull and an impending lawsuit. Are owners of stores becoming frugal, or is this a hidden agenda from some twisted cigarette Nazi group? One would imagine they would be helping our environmental fruitcakes. I do not like to litter, but I am not going to take one for the team and put it out with my hand. Nor, am I going to step on it and pick it up. Does anybody have any idea what germs are lurking around our public sidewalks and roadways?

Florida is not the only state that has laws against throwing your lit cigarette out the car window. If it is not lit, then it is a simple $100.00 fine, but if the thing is lit, then it could be a misdemeanor. That is why it is a dumb idea to throw your lit cigarette out the window at nighttime. Cops can see the sparks flying around like an exploding pack of firecrackers. However, the misdemeanor applies to any lit object heaved from your speeding vehicle. So, be careful if you are throwing out a joint, cigar, bong, crack-pipe or your Ritalin-starved baby brother.

I hate when people give me a dirty look when I light a cigarette in places that are legal to smoke. I could be fifty feet away lighting a cigarette with my back to a 30MPH wind, only to turn around to see some clown giving me a look of contempt. You know the look; it is the look of some mongoloid shaking their head back and fourth. The next time I see that, I am putting my cigarette out on his or her forehead.

During the fist week of July 2005, San Francisco enacted an outdoor smoking ban. The law banned smoking from parks, squares, gardens and playing fields under their city park control. There are approximately 250 parks in the *City by the Bay*, but to add one more sign in their arsenal of ridiculous signs is as ridiculous as the smoking ban. Here are some of their dim-witted signs that dot their precious little parks and how I understand them.

Pick up and remove dog waste- My dog's crap, or any crap I see?

Leash your dog(s) - They do not make one in her size!

Don't leave your dog unattended - I was hoping somebody would take her.

Control excessive barking and noise - How do you control noise?

Prevent digging and destructive behavior - Is ripping an arm off someone destructive?

Keep your dog's vaccinations and license current – Roger that!

I don't want to go on a rant, but that's what dogs do! They bark, run around like Kool-Aide babies, dig holes, and crap. Dog owners should have a house with enough property for a large dog and a one bedroom flat for an ankle-biter. Remember, Fido has no say so in the matter. Why have a dog and bring it to a park? Perhaps all the dogs commiserate with each other by barking, "You think cigarette butts stink, well check this out!"

I'm sure San Francisco can find other problems besides worrying if someone is smoking a cigarette in one of their parks. Hey, thimble-heads, instead of handing out free needles and condoms to your close-knit society, your tribal leaders should hand out cigarettes. I have always wondered if drugs or their *yearly leather brigade-parade* is worse than smoking. San Francisco has some huge problems, but they're worried about residents smoking in a park?

San Francisco is left of left on the political scene. According to the San Francisco Chronicle in 2005, Recreation and Park Department Supervisor, Michela Alioto-Pier said, "The impetus for this was the amount of cigarette butts we were finding on the ground." That is what cigarette smokers do at a park Michela. They leave their butts on the ground, but thanks for the big word. By her admission, there appears to be cigarette smokers in San Francisco. She further added, "They leach toxins into our groundwater." That is the least of the crap that is going into their ground water; no pun intended.

A bee sting is a toxin. A toxin is a poisonous substance created by living cells. How does the word toxin apply to cigarette butts? Are living cells from cigarette butts starting to scare you? That would be the least of my worries if I drank San Franciscan tap water. Did you read your 2005 water report? Most large cities have this little thing called a sewage treatment plant and the stuff listed is the normal nauseating ingredients one would find in such a facility. Don't forget about pesticides and herbicides, let alone what else goes down the drains in San Francisco. I would rather swallow the juice extracted from 1,000 cartons of cigarettes. I would be worrying about saltwater intrusion if I lived there, but let your water experts assess the facts.

In 2006, Calabasas, an area of Los Angeles I know quite well, enacted their own outdoor smoking ban. It prevents people from smoking on sidewalks, parks, bus stops, outdoor cafes, condominium pool decks and other places. God, I am so glad I left that state. American Nonsmokers' Rights Foundation naturally supported that ordinance. Who is going to enforce the ordinance in San Francisco or Calabasas? California has a hard time controlling crime, but they appear to be hell-bent on putting forth efforts to stop smoking everywhere.

According to the FBI, there were 6,533 violent crimes in San Francisco in 2006. In fact, there were 86 murders alone. The Golden State had 2,000 murders in 2006 and 7,500 rapes. I know Calabasas is about the size of a raison, but they had 24 violent crimes in the same period. Regardless, are these buffoons really worried about cigarette smokers?

California had 393,000 robberies in 2006, but these two cities are worried about secondhand smoke? There are hundreds of unsolved murder cases in San Francisco alone, so why aren't the crackpots trying to find the killers. After all, nobody has died from secondhand smoke, but people have died from murderers. Who knows, perhaps the killers are still in their tribe, or maybe they escaped. The worst-case scenario is having a killer still lurking in the San Franciscan tribe while continuing to smoke in the park with his man-eating pit-bull that does not stop barking while taking a steamer.

Oh well, I shouldn't pick on California too much, because they do a fine job of embarrassing themselves on a repeated basis. If I ever move back, I would be more concerned about having a celebrity hack me to pieces than care if my neighbor was smoking on the sidewalk.

An estimated 100-million people in this country caught either a cold or flu in 2008. Thousands of people will die from influenza; in fact, more people will die from the common flu in 2009 then people with aids in the US. These are disturbing statistics, so what are we going to do about it? I think San Francisco should make everybody who catches a cold or flu wear a little surgical mask. This would greatly reduce the transmission each year, and it would be for a noble cause. Moreover, it would give us another reason to laugh, because the city would look like a freak show, yet it would slow down unnecessary deaths, unlike the supposed secondhand smoke.

The world's problem about AIDS is not mine. I think twenty years of awareness is enough and anybody who wants to volunteer to strap condoms on the natives in our remote jungles can do so. Perhaps this could be a lucrative industry for the short people.

Lastly, how does Las Vegas get away with all of the smoking that goes on in that town? I do not think ASH or any other nonsmoking group can affect them. Three things go hand-in-hand with prostitutes in Las Vegas; smoking, gambling and drinking. I hate when I am the first one at a blackjack table and light up, only to have people show up during my smoking prowess and start complaining. Hey, I was there first, so go some place else. I smoke in their elevators, restaurants or anywhere I want to smoke. What happens in Las Vegas stays in Las Vegas. Las Vegas appears to be a smoker's sanctuary and I will continue to fund that charity as long as I live.

I am considerate to those who do not like cigarette smoke for whatever reason. I only have contempt for those who think they are going to get secondhand lung cancer or feel it is their obligatory duty to annoy my day by shoving their ideology, comments and actions towards me. I hate some people's cologne and perfume, but I have to put up with that stench in an enclosed building all day long. What rights do I have? In case nobody knows, there are plenty of carcinogens in that stuff, so apparently nobody cares about people getting cancer while having to smell used dishwater all day.

Special Interest Groups
– Traffic cops

Everybody is an expert, or at least pretend to be, in wanting to help protect us from the impending dangers of driving. There are groups called Advocates for Highway and Auto Safety, American Highway Users Alliance, The Center for Auto Safety and Citizens for Roadway Safety. Good God, is there that many problems on our roadways? We have to keep in mind how many stationary items that stupid drivers hit each year. Thousands of people die every year by hitting trees, fire hydrants, telephone poles, parked cars, etc.

How does one hit a telephone pole? How one hits a pole while driving sober, with no other vehicles within one mile, no medical problems, or some type of mechanical malfunction is a mystery to me. The answer is because the driver is a moron. Unless he or she suddenly died tragically before the impact, there is no other answer. I can imagine some of these scenarios actually happened:

A young male was punching the one-eyed clown while rocking-out to "Pour Some Sugar on Me" when he crashed into a real power pole.

A young female decided to flash some construction workers and didn't see the other parked cement truck.

If someone dropped a cigarette between their legs, I'm sure it's possible the last thing they she saw when they looked up was a pole. Oh well, at least they didn't burn their privates.

People with a normal sized brain would change the radio station if Eminem came over the airwaves. However, look up every once in awhile when you're trying to find something decent.

The list is long, but distinguished. I can type scenarios like this all day long and probably get each one right. I don't care if there are 1,000 advocacy groups for highway safety, it would not protect these types of morons from perishing. These rocket scientists reinforce the ideology that only the strong shall survive.

What is the impact to our socioeconomic makeup if we lose dumb drivers? I am glad they are off the road, because it lessens my odds of being pegged by one of them. Any additional amount of road signs would prove useless to these types of drivers. We are always going to have a knucklehead standing up in the backseat of a convertible dancing to YMCA, sober or under the influence. Therefore, do we need to have Watch out for low-hanging branch signs dotting the highways?

Some road signs have proven to be of great benefit to all drivers. The problem is, that some people don't read them, cannot read them, or they think too hard. When a posted sign states, *Bridge out ahead*, that means hit your damn breaks quickly. I could imagine that some of these neophyte drivers are actually thinking the following:

Oh, it can't be the next bridge, because I just went over it last month. I wonder if it's the other bridge right after I normally exit. Well, I saw a car coming past me on the other side, so it can't be this bridge. Wait, that car was on the other side because this is a divided expansion bridge. That is one example of either thinking too hard or trying to over rationalize a road sign.

There is a group in Long Island, New York who not only wants more Deer Crossing signs, but they also want them illuminated at night. Wow, these are such caring people as not to want to harm any of their fellow village idiots, but also have a big heart for God's animals. Hey morons, would you snap out of it! Deer cannot read, nor can any other animal you whiny little worms. Do you think deer are only going to cross where the posted signs exist? Are the intentions for illumination for the driver or the deer? Either way, you people are freaky. Why do you want more signs for deer?

Did you ever think a deer or any other animal could run out of the trees one-half mile before a sign? There is nothing you can do about hitting a large animal or a tribe of little pygmies running across a highway. You are either going to plow into them and survive or not. Moreover, there should only be minor damage if someone plows into pygmies. For the record, I heard if you spray Pam on your front bumper prior to pygmy season, it causes them to career off the bumper and not leave such nasty dents. Besides, if you're going to erect more signs, be aware of the people that oppose billboards. They don't like signs.

These are your basic freaky people. *Billboard Advertisers are Idiots* and a plethora of similar groups want billboards to go away like dinosaurs. I think it would be unfair for me to refer to them as retarded, therefore I think the word drool-cup wearing morons is more fitting. It is a visual form of advertising, but that's the same thing as a TV commercial. These groups think billboards are polluting our beautiful concrete jungles, as well as our mind. Yet, they don't care if I have to endure another Viagra commercial. Apparently, it is okay to look at concrete, graffiti, gold teeth, and bums, but not billboards. I don't notice billboards, because I'm too busy driving! I only look for them when I'm in search of something, such as a gas station. It's hard enough to drive when I look to my side and notice some sweat-hog on the back of a Harley. Some people are ugly too, just like billboards, houses, and a herd of undernourished cows that dot our highways.

Billboards have been dotting our roadways prior to the famous Burma Shave advertisement that started in1925; however, Burma Shave made them popular. The California Supreme Court struck down a ban on billboards as early as 1909. Former San Diego Mayor Pete Wilson tried his best to get rid of them, but failed like a Chargers attempt to make it to the Super Bowl. I liked Pete only because he was a Republican and a decent Governor of my home state. Yet, what was he thinking in trying to help ban billboards in San Diego? Come on Pete, you couldn't see all the illegal aliens running across the border? Were they using billboards for camouflage? That should have been your priority, not sign control.

Regardless, the notion that billboards are a distraction is pure rhetoric. How many people are plowing into the sides of cars or fences after they claimed they were reading a billboard? There is no evidence that proves any correlation between billboards and accidents. If there is, then what are these dumb drivers looking at for so long?

If you have a stuttering driver trying to pronounce, *Waffle-House Ahead* to his or her deaf-mute passenger, then I may see a problem. We have mechanical and digital billboards all over our highways and I love them. How else would I know where the next McDonalds is located, guess?

What if I exited an off-ramp where deer were playing in an oasis of beautiful pine trees, only to discover a group of gypsy sodomites waiting for me at the bottom? I would be gang-raped and humiliated, but a McDonalds sign would have prevented that unnecessary event. I want to know where McDonalds, Hooters and gas stations are located when I'm traveling. Do billboard haters have E.S.P. or some yuppie little navigational system that tells them where to exit for the next Starbucks? Well, I have neither and that's the way I like it.

Moreover, billboards are not located in subdivisions or housing developments. I see more crap than I care to see before I notice my first billboard. I see fruit-loops walking around my neighborhood, kids running in the street, ugly people, cars resting on cement blocks and other related eyesores. They do not bother me in the least, because I find them entertaining, especially my neighbor with schizophrenia. This poor sap is slapping and swatting at invisible things all day long.

Before I hit the interstate, I notice moving, or mobile billboards. I see vans listed with everything imaginable, as well as tractor-trailers with advertising on them. What if you're waiting for the cable guy and he shows up in a plain white van? How do you know it's the cable guy, unless the van is labeled? Cable companies have their logo to promote advertisement as well as identification. The same holds true for plumbers, telephone companies, etc.

Does it really irritate anyone to see a tractor-trailer advertising a product? I bet people who think this type of advertising is wrong are merely jealous. What about NASCAR owners who have tractor-trailers advertising their drivers, as well as the products they endorse? Do these groups of billboard haters dislike those as well? If they do, I think their cause is useless and proves that jealousy is once again raising its ugly head. I would have my face plastered on every sign in America if I had Bill Gate's money. The meek shall inherit zip, so get over it.

Therefore, the bloody wankers who think billboards should disappear apparently approve of the nonsensical material that airs on television. It is impossible to argue with anybody with that rationale.

There is actually a group starting to whine about hybrid cars. Their logic for disliking hybrid cars is because they think they put a deaf pedestrian at a disadvantage. Some hybrid cars are extremely quiet, but that is why a deaf person uses his or her sight before crossing the road.

As a country, we continue to try our best to shut these people up, but they are like flies. As soon as you swat one, here comes another. That's because there is another group claiming that hybrid vehicles are lethal for blind pedestrians, even though there is no indication a blind person was mowed over by one of these vehicles.

Blind people have a very acute sense of hearing. They rely on this conventional human sense more than any other due to their lack of sight. Drivers see people, whether the pedestrian is blind or not. They may not see them until they are in their rearview mirror, but accidents unfortunately happen.

What I think is strange is that I'm not hearing anything from people wanting to do anything for these people suffering from these unspeakable human deficiencies. Naturally, nobody can tell if a pedestrian is deaf or not. However, for the sake of arguing, suppose a deaf person was wearing a t-shirt with large embroidered letters stating, I AM DEAF. Okay, so now what does the driver do? I do not think hitting the horn would work, but somebody will figure it out. Obviously, any smart deaf person would have those words printed on the front and backsides of their t-shirt.

I understand the notion that we cannot protect every citizen who has a physical or mental impairment from the dangers of vehicles. Hybrid cars do not compose the majority of the vehicles on our roadways. As an example, what does somebody who stutters say to an oncoming 68 Chevelle, "Luh-luh-luh-luh oookkk-out, ssttsttststsstt"- **Crash!** By the time he or she comes out of their brief coma, their next word would be, "wha-wha-wha-wha-wha the fah-fah-fah-fah-fah-fah-fah!"

There are citizens who suffer from Cotard's disorder, or better known as walking corpse syndrome. No, I am not making this up. We also have people who are sleep driving. Sleep driving is on the rise because of Ambien, or that's what a class-action suit is alleging. So, who would be at fault if an Ambien-popping fool ran over a person who suffers from walking corpse syndrome? Now that would be a funny trial if the person who got ran over survived. I would imagine the proceedings would be as follows:

Plaintiff's Lawyer: *"Your honor, my client has Cotard's syndrome and was ran over by the defendant."*

Judge: *"If your client is a retard, then he has no idea what happened."*

Plaintiff's Lawyer: *"I'm sorry your honor, but he is not a retard. He suffers from Cotard's Syndrome, which is something different."*

Judge: *"Before I address the defense, please explain to the court what the difference is between the two. I am not familiar with Cotard's syndrome."*

Plaintiff's Lawyer: *"Cotard's Syndrome is a disease in which a person thinks they are dead."*

Judge: *"That sounds like a retard to me. What is the defense's position?"*

Judge: As he points to the defense counsel says, *"Did your client run over that retard?"*

Defense Lawyer: *"My client was unaware of what happened, because he was sleeping behind the wheel."*

Judge: *"Was he intoxicated?"*

Defense Lawyer: *"No your honor, he was on Ambien."*

Judge: *"Does your client know that Ambien makes you drowsy? It's like drinking a half a bottle of rum for Christ's sake."*

Defense Lawyer: *"That may be true, but he was unaware of the side affects. He is part of the litigation against the makers of Ambien."*

Judge: After pointing to the bailiff says, *"Get these four retards out of my courtroom!"*

Bailiff: *"Four retards your honor?"*

Judge: *"I stand corrected. Make that five, because you're leaving too Rusty."*

One of these websites dedicated to keeping the traffic machine alive and well listed the Top 10 reasons why your state needs an all-rider motorcycle helmet law. Interestingly, there were only seven reasons listed on the page. Here are some of the seven reasons:

1) Helmet Laws Save Lives: "Motorcycle helmets are 37% effective in preventing motorcyclist deaths and 67 percent in preventing brain injuries." *Well, to me that indicates that 63% of the times helmets are ineffective of saving lives and 33% ineffective in preventing brain injuries. I guess you have a better chance of surviving a crash without a helmet.*

2) In 2006, 4,810 motorcycle riders died in crashes. *Maybe so, but according to the D.O.T., 1,878 of those deaths were single vehicle crashes. Moreover, 41% had a BAC of over .08%. I wonder if the other 1,108 riders hit a telephone pole or parked car.*

3) <u>Helmets do not increase the likelihood of spinal injury or crash.</u> *Perhaps that's why riders don't wear helmets? Who wrote that line?*

I can give you my reasons why motorcycle riders don't wear helmets.

1) Nobody looks cool riding a Harley wearing a helmet, unless the brain-bucket is a Viking helmet.

2) If you force anyone to do anything, their natural recourse is to rebel.

3) Most importantly, who cares? Gary Busey healed nicely. More importantly, I didn't see any further degradation of his mental faculties after his spill. He appeared to be the same to me, before, during and after his coma.

Another website dedicated to auto safety claims guardrails kill. I hate to split hairs, but I've never seen a guardrail kill anybody. The fact of the matter is trees, telephone poles, power poles, parked cars or fire hydrants do not kill people. People hit them; therefore, stationary items do not chase, or hunt and attack people.

Can engineers improve every stationary item that people hit? Probably, but I don't want my fire-hydrant wrapped in rubber tires in case my house is on fire and I'm not cutting a tree down that surrounds *dead man's curve.* It wasn't the pole's fault. Is there anybody willing to take accountability into their lives?

This same site also lists some interesting car crashes. One was a woman who spilled a cup of hot chocolate and caused her to swerve! I believe it was at this point the killer guardrail attacked. The woman spilled some hot chocolate. Where is the accountability? I had to get off this site, because it was a little too freaky when I started reading about the bogus lawsuit. Do the guardrails have any rights? Where's Johnny Cochran when you need him?

American Highway Users Alliance is a massive website. They have a lot of material related to driving associated issues. They allegedly lobbied for the 2008 $40-Billion DOT highway budget. If I had boatloads of money to give to each Congress member, I could probably have our National Symbol switched to the Golden Arches. Nothing is hard to accomplish with money.

I am not insinuating they bribed, coerced or even condone such practices of greasing the palms of our greedy little politicians, but politicians have lined their pockets from other charitable contributions. Can anybody name one elected position that hasn't taken a contribution? It could be your local mayor, or even worse, your county coroner.

This site, along with others, discusses the safety or lack thereof regarding our bridges. If I read one more article about our bridges falling down, I'm going to gag. Shortly after the 35W bridge collapse in St. Paul, MN, virtually every reporter decided to write about the degradation of our bridges and the nauseating statistics to support their stories. A slew of reporters rattled off statistics as if they built every bridge in the US. Almost every article cites the statistic of our country having 600,000 bridges. What they failed to tell anyone is that according to the D.O.T., a bridge is twenty feet or longer and does not include railroad trusses.

Therefore, when reporters cite there are 78,000 bridges that are in need of repair, my question to them is, can they point them out for me? At least give me the names, so I can feel that I am safe. Here is some information to help people decide if they think our bridges are falling down.

More people have died from building bridges, as opposed to people having a miserable commute on their way home. Approximately thirty-seven men died while building the Brooklyn Bridge. I must use the word approximate, because that is the least known amount. An additional eleven men died while building the Golden Gate Bridge. In the past three decades, approximately ninety-five people died from bridge collapses in the US. However, I can't include the people who died of bridge collapses because a barge slammed into it! It does not matter if the captain was drinking, sleeping or winking at his first mate; those deaths happened because a traveling object hit a stationary object. Eighty-one out of the ninety-five deaths in the last few decades were victims of battering rams, and not faulty bridges.

Potholes on the other hand, put people into vicarious predicaments and situations on a daily basis. A bicyclist can experience a *death-wobble*, which are funny to watch, but not to the bicyclist wearing pink shorts. He bought them in hot pink, but after a horrifying *death-wobble*, also known as a headshake in motorcycle racing, the pink shorts will reveal a new racing stripe. Potholes are everywhere in this country. They are also known as urban acne, hollows, caverns and chuckholes. Some are so large, I think a more apropos name would be *troll-hole*. I have actually seen some larger than Rosie O'Donnell's head to give you a reference.

If you hit a good-sized pothole in a car at a high rate of speed, it is very easy to blow two tires in one shot. Most cities or municipalities will pay for damages, but you have to go through massive amounts of red tape to collect your money. These potholes will not only wreck the outside of your car, but will violate its interior when your coffee goes flying all over the place.

You can expect potholes to show themselves after a bad winter in our snow-belt states, as a result from frost heave. Frost heave occurs after the freezing and thawing of soil. Therefore, after a nasty and hellish winter in Akron, Ohio, it is common to find your car airborne after you hit a little hill caused by frost heave. I just hope the landing is better than how the poor Mustang landed in the movie Bullet.

However, I cannot rationalize the notion that people sue when they trip over a pothole. How does one not see a pothole? Does a seeing eye-dog trip in a pothole? The answer is no, they do not. For Christ's sake, a normal dog has four legs, but they don't trip and people only have two. One would think that percentages would dictate that four legs would cause for a higher tripping rate, as opposed to two legs. No, it's just a fact that people are stupid and not paying attention.

We have all seen morons trip or stumble on their two feet. If you don't believe me, plop your butt on a bench in a mall and watch. People are tripping all over the place. There are no potholes in tile and there is no little midgets running around tripping people. People are too busy to notice the ground, but think they're smart enough to notice a 10% discount at Radio Shack. These are the dumb people in the world and they should not be entitled to punitive, compensatory or any other damages if they trip on a pothole. I don't care if they blackout after they sustain a concussion. Accidents happen and accountability should come into play, as opposed to lawyers.

There are too many cars on the road to fill every pothole, however local government workers need to get off their butts and fix the severe ones. They know which ones are bad based on how many people call their 1-800-FIX-THE-HOLE complaint number. If they factor how many complaints and compare it to how many drivers take that road on a daily basis, then it shouldn't be that hard to get them filled before another brown stripe appears on a pair of pink bicycle shorts.

There appears to be many groups pushing for the installation of LED traffic lights. The logic behind their crusade is saving individual State's electric bills, reducing traffic accidents and the reduction of greenhouse emissions. Along with the installation of LED traffic lights, some of these same groups are pushing for better traffic control management. The example is waiting in a car too long before the light changes for the driver to proceed. These same whiners complain if they have to wait more than two minutes at a McDonald's drive-through.

According to the California Energy Commission, the LED light lasts five times longer than a regular halogen or incandescent bulb, but it will cost California approximately $50,000,000 to retrofit their worst intersections. If California had to rob a bank to get the money to do this, it will save approximately $8,000,000 per year in electricity, so the ROI will take approximately six years. The same study conducted in 2002 said this would save one megawatt of power.

This is enough power to feed approximately 10,000 homes. The easiest thing to do would be to kick everybody out who lives in Folsom. However, with the daily influx of illegal aliens and people moving into California on a daily basis, each city is growing every year. Regardless, my little environmentalist friends see this as a goldmine, because less carbon dioxide will be used by the existing power plants.

The pro LED movement has taken a life form of its own, just as any project in California. Other benefits by switching to LED traffic lights, as opposed to incandescent bulbs, are the following:

The lights would be more beneficial in fog, because they burn brighter. I don't care if the lights had strobe lights and disco balls dangling from them, because people are still going to run red lights. If you tell people they will be brighter in fog, then the little mutant drivers will drive faster thinking they can see them in time.

One interesting thing they are doing is installing little speakers on the poles for blind people. An audible voice will prompt the person and their seeing-eye dog to let them know it is okay to cross. I think this is a marvelous idea. Yet, one would think they would also install a loud audible device warning people in wheelchairs.

Who is looking out after the cripples? The technology in video, audio and sensors have dramatically increased over the years. We need to make all citizens safer when attempting to cross a street. If we mounted adequate sensors and video cameras to monitor each intersection, speakers could emit the following commands in a clarion call, thus causing citizens to take the appropriate action:

"Roll Faster, faster, you can do it" is a command for people in wheelchairs when a sensor and video detect an impending impact.

"Pedal faster" or *"Slam on the brakes"* are commands for people on bicycles.

"Look straight ahead at all times" is a command for married men who turn around to watch a woman's butt as they cross paths in an intersection. If he does not listen, then the automatic sensing device will call the wife's cell phone and display the video taken at the intersection. Let him explain his way out of this one.

"Drop the cane and make a run for it gramps" is a command for a senior citizen who does not see the Mac truck barreling down on him. Naturally, a fully matured adult hobbling around in depends cannot bust-out in a mad sprint for a myriad of reasons. It is at this point; his cane will careen off the first LED light and continue to take out two more LED lights. This would cost the city plenty of money. In addition, does anybody realize how expensive a hand-carved cane cost these days?

Moreover, I do not care if they retrofit our current traffic bulb to a LED, or even a kerosene lamp. For some reason, they cannot manage to hang any sort of traffic light, without me having to put my neck at a 90-degree angle to see when the light changes. Until they stop hanging lights in vicarious positions relative to where the white line is located, I don't care if they put a monkey in the intersection directing traffic. I am sick and tired of dislocating my C-6 and C-7 vertebrae while I am at a complete stop.

However, there was an interesting article written in the same period, proposing an alterative way to save money in energy costs in California. The crux of the article is building more substations. The authors' proposal of building more substations and implementing newer generators would save California an estimated $500,000,000 per year in energy costs. The environmentalists are attacking that study, simply because there would be more generators and those little beasts would be emitting more pollutants into the air. When was the last time anybody went to China and breathed their cloud of coal?

We have it made in the US when it comes to air quality, but it's never good enough for the complainers. I've never seen one environmentalist in this country using a rickshaw. That would be a good way to put the homeless to work and reduce carbon dioxide. However, don't hire a deaf person to pull your rickshaw without bringing a whip. Has anyone ever tried barking orders to the backside of a deaf person? It doesn't work, but most people understand a whip. In this case, the driver is either going to speed up or stop.

I think we should stop making automobiles and use horse and buggy for transportation. We could also use elephants, camels, Chinese junk, Pedi-cabs and samlors. Why should the Amish have all the fun? We should all join them. All we need to do is wear suspenders, grow a beard and change our names to Zeke or Ezekiel. We could all move to Pennsylvania and sell our hand-beaten butter over the Internet. I don't understand that logic at all. They have high-speed internet and no cars? Wow, how do those slow-thinking people survive?

The main problem lies within the amount of vehicles on our roadways today. The amount of vehicles is not in proportion with the amount of available lanes, thus gridlock. There is nothing worse than sitting idly, whether it is on an interstate or at an intersection. Yet, we should not complain if we have to sit idly on the interstate due to an accident involving a tractor-trailer and fifteen cars.

Moreover, people need to stop whining because they have to wait at a light. The same problem exists because there are too many vehicles. It doesn't matter if you install little cameras to help manage the changing of the light, because you can't have green lights all of the time no matter what you do.

There are other things to consider, such as trains, bridges, accidents ahead, etc. What about the poor sap who needs to make a left? Should he or she have to suffer because they are the only car in the lane wanting to make a left? Every city has been suffering from traffic since the sixties, but virtually every city avoided the inevitable. Now that we all have to suffer, suck it up and deal with it. When was the last time anybody drove down Las Vegas Blvd on a Friday night? Every tweak imaginable is on that stretch of highway, so now the locals take the back-roads to get themselves home or to work in a reasonable timeframe.

Orlando is bulging at the seams like a fat woman in tight jeans. Every city needs to improve their highway system before it becomes a disaster. It's never too late, but the country needs to put some effort into it. The Army and Marines can put together a bridge in one hour to get their tanks and equipment across a river, but we can't figure out how to manage our traffic infrastructure? The Army not only builds bridges, but they also shoot at the enemy at the same time. It appears all we want to do is whine about traffic and worry about how many pollutants we are putting in the air. At the end of the day, does anybody really care? Is all the stimulus money spent? Besides Louisiana, where did all of our money go?

When I'm motoring down the highway, I throw out my beer cans and flick my cigarettes out the window. I'm keeping bums happy and the street sweeper gainfully employed. If nobody littered, do you know how many people would be unemployed? Furthermore, every beer or pop can is worth good money and the bums could use the money. We have already made our intersections into retail establishments.

Only in America can we expect some group soliciting for charitable contributions at an intersection. You know the type I'm talking about, because they're all the same. They walk around with orange buckets with some name on it written with a black marker. In addition, anyone can buy oranges, grapefruits, Chiclets and gold watches at an intersection too. Apparently, law enforcement is too busy eradicating smokers to notice that our intersections look like the Mexican border as you enter California.

I don't see the other problems that people claim to exist when discussing roadway safety. Our bridges are not falling down and as long as people are behind the wheel of a vehicle, accidents will happen. As our population continues to grow, the amount of accidents will raise exponentially. Who cares if people don't wear motorcycle helmets? Only the people riding a motorcycle should be concerned. The excuse that it costs taxpayers too much money for an uninsured Evel Knievel is ludicrous. If anybody did his or her math, figure out how much taxpayers spend on teen pregnancy. A few thousand brain operations resulting from crashes on motorcycles fail in comparison.

Morons hitting stationary objects are included in the statistics provided by several sources to publicize their claim that we need more safety on our roadways. Nothing can help stupidity and accidents are just that, an accident. Drunk drivers kill more people than guardrails. Cell phones, DVD players, and laptop computers do not kill, but the twits driving while using those devices are to blame. I suggest we implement the following:

<u>Buses:</u> Do busses have to stop every 100 yards? If you are the unfortunate driver who is stuck behind one of these germ incubators, then you're going to suffer a nervous breakdown. Each bus stop should be one mile apart. This will allow for the drivers behind the bus to merge over. I feel like throwing a rock at people who have to disembark from the bus right in front of their place of employment. Normally, these people are wearing a fast food or Best Buy uniform. These subhuman species could afford to walk off the extra weight and quit blocking traffic. All bus riders need to do in order to help our societal woes regarding traffic is board the Ralph Kramden express fifteen minutes earlier.

<u>People who blow through stop signs or red lights:</u> Once the middle section of a car has passed over the white line, a laser beam should have it vaporized. There would be nothing left except the shadow of the car and a pair of pink fuzzy dice. If the laser prevented a tragedy, then the car and its driver would never return. If the driver hit a pedestrian or another car, then he or she would wake up in their car in Akron, Ohio. If this is a wakeup call, then mission accomplished. Nobody should want to know what hell is like.

<u>Swerving:</u> Install sensors onto our interstates that would detect people who are swerving. If any of their tires hit the sensors mounted on the white-lines twice within one minute, then their car becomes a shadow as well. There would be nothing left except the outline depicting the possible model. This would help police who are locating missing people. There are no second chances for drunks or people with no regard for others around them. Akron would not be a deterrent, so they never get a second chance.

People who can't merge: This is one of the easiest maneuvers for a driver to perform. All a driver has to do while merging onto an interstate is one of two things, slow down or speed up! I am always courteous to the morons around me, so I wave people in front of me who wish to merge, because they're going too slow and can't decide whether to go slower or risk it by hitting the gas pedal. They remind me of the Yankees' outfielders who run towards home plate to catch a ball and then realize the ball is over their heads like the space shuttle.

They look at me in their side mirror as though I'm swatting at a bee in my vehicle. However, there are aggressive idiots who have to merge also. They either cut you off, or stay clear to the right and see how far they can get before they have to merge into backed-up traffic. The person who cuts somebody off should fall prey to the laser. The dimwits who think they can pass several cars that have been patiently waiting in line should have a metal pole pop up through the ground, like a hydraulic barrier. It will ruin his or her day, but at least they will survive. I don't think they can financially afford to repeat this stupid little game.

How many times have you been traveling at a speed of 35MPH on the interstate, only to find out it's someone older than Arlen Specter at the wheel causing the traffic jam? The old man normally has a scared look on his face as though he's racing in the Daytona 500. The only thing the old driver has in common with the Daytona 500 is the color of the UPS car. That color happens to match the stripe in his underwear that he just created after merging onto the interstate.

In most states, old drivers can drive until they get into an accident. That's kind of like waiting for your spastic child to get an F in physical education. In other words, it's going to happen sooner than later. They should revoke the license of anybody once they reach the age of 75, as well as flunk a spastic kid on his first day of P.E. The government should pay for free luxurious limousine services to people once they turn 75.

This is for two reasons: My parents and in-laws are older than seventy-five and still drive, but most importantly, anybody who can prove they worked for fifty years, as well as paid their taxes deserves this privilege. Besides, I'll be there someday myself, and I'm looking forward to a limousine hauling my bass boat to the Perdido River. The river that borders Florida and Alabama, for the last 55 miles as it meanders into the Gulf of Mexico, epitomizes tranquility. If I don't catch any fish, the limo driver will also be paid to help fabricate any fishing stories. My female driver would have long blonde hair, bait my hooks, open my beer, and wear a halter-top. In addition to that, wait.....the wife may read this part too.

Special Interest Groups – Animal Rights

There are at least fourteen groups on the Internet asking for donations to help in their crusades for the protection of animals in one form or another. Some are to the extreme, just as in any special interest group, and some are just plain ridiculous. I know animals perform in zoos, keep me fed and their hides make great coats and wallets. I love to fish, hunt and trap, but some of these groups apparently disagree. I would not equate myself to a Michael Vick, but flushing a goldfish down the toilet is funny to watch, let alone watching a monkey masturbate in a zoo. I think the sick people in the world are the ones who don't laugh at monkeys slinging their poop or masturbating in public. People are arrested for that all the time, but monkeys have a safe zone, and it's called a cage.

Most zoos keep their animals better fed than what the critter could scrounge-up in its natural habitat. However, nobody can even agree to disagree on whether animals live longer in a zoo or in the wild. Who really cares? If an elephant drops dead in a zoo, then get another one. Anybody can switch out an Indian elephant with another one because nobody would notice the difference. Besides, if India continues to experience the wrath of *elephants gone wild*, they would be more than happy to give us another pachyderm.

Approximately 400 Indians die per year from irate elephants, so they would be more than happy to repopulate our zoos. Elephants are not your typical *gentle giants* of the wild. The African elephants are just as mean. They kill villagers and poor tourists quite often. Can you imagine saving all of your money to go to the Serengeti only to receive a throttling from something other than a blowgun?

What if you were talking to your local Dell Computer representative named *Mike*, only to hear him scream for his life as a pack of elephants comes ripping through his thatched hut? Actually, that would be funny in a macabre sort of way. It would really be eerie if your cursor kept moving until Mike succumbed to those nasty set of ivories. I wonder what would be worse, having your face impaled by tusks or having Flavor Flav biting you with his gold grille. He could be the last person alive not to evolve from his original species, which was the gold-grilled, saber-toothed, Bridgette-Eating wild thing. I need to rinse my brain with scope, just so I can get the thoughts of her taste out of my head.

How many times does a person go to the same zoo? I lived close to the Los Angeles zoo and went three times my whole life. They could keep switching elephants and I would never notice the difference. They all look the same. Besides, if an elephant can live to be thirty-fifty years in captivity, then how many times do you think the same person is going to see the same elephant? I have other things to do with my life, like watching elephants in a circus. I would imagine they don't walk on their hind legs wearing pink tutus in their natural habitat, but a circus isn't natural either. Other than Carrot Top, when was the last time somebody saw a clown walking down the street?

Do you recall the last time Siegfried and Roy played with a tiger on stage? I seriously doubt if Roy is willing to rip a jackal carcass away from a hungry lion in Africa or scratch the chin of a malnourished tiger in Siberia. Those savages kill people too, in or out of a zoo, just like an elephant. Most of the natives in those countries only have their feet for protection, so it's hard to outrun a tiger bearing down on you like a tomahawk cruise missile. Although it's hard to stomach watching a tiger chasing down its food on National Geographic, try swallowing a spoonful of tapioca pudding if they show a tiger ripping a native's head off his shoulders.

An African male wearing only war paint and a pair of 1975 blue-colored Nike shoes cannot outrun a hungry cheetah, nor could his small son with a bloated belly. I don't think it would be funny at all to watch a cheetah running in slow motion on National Geographic only to find out its target was a father and son running for their lives. I don't want to see a look of disgust, angst and pure terror in the eyeballs of the fleet-footed natives. Well, fleet-footed may be the wrong term in this scenario. The pace of the father and son would match the speed of a Frisbee thrown into the wind.

Before I mention such groups as PETA, Animal Legal Defense Fund and American Humane, it is only appropriate to continue with zoos, simply because I find them fascinating. Where else can you see killer whales doing back flips and seals balancing balls on their nose? An adult film has girls balancing balls on their chins, but seals don't have chins, so it doesn't count. Zoos or a park that have animals to entertain us is not animal abuse, because it cuts down on deaths to natives and saves us from traveling to third-world countries. Why should I risk my life in Africa to get a glimpse of a silverback gorilla when I can go to a zoo and pound on the glass windows and irritate the big fellow?

The whole notion that zoos are unfair to animals is insane logic. Animals eat better, receive medical attention and their daily needs are met. Whoever thinks a three-legged jackal has fun and a longer life in the Serengeti is listening to the *other side*. Wild animals maim or kill people in their natural habitat, or in a stage show in Las Vegas. They are unpredictable because they are wild. Therefore, whenever somebody requires plastic surgery and a trauma team to heal them, it is because wild animals are just that, wild. This is inclusive of all parks, including the ones where you can safely stay in your car and see the big animals. In this case, the visitor and their car normally require bodywork after they take the tour.

God put animals on our planet for several reasons and one of them is for our enjoyment. Who wants to go to Siberia, Sri Lanka, Africa or Antarctica for any reason, let alone look at their animals? Antarctica has nothing but penguins, so we had to bring the penguins here so we can watch them slide down artificial rockwork. If we watch Discovery, we can watch the sharks eat them. At Sea World for example, the poor little penguin can frolic around inside a pool with both their eyes looking forward, as opposed to having one of them looking behind their butt. They don't have to worry about a zookeeper throwing in an orca as a practical joke. I like polar bears swimming in pools at zoos, but if anybody thinks I'm going to the North Pole so I can get my head ripped-off by one of those beasts, they're crazy.

Animals don't do much in their natural habitat, so it would be terribly boring to watch a bear hibernate. Bears don't hibernate in a zoo, because they eat every day. Who wants to go to Alaska and watch some grizzly snoozing for five months? The only fun in Alaska is trying to keep up with the natives in the local saloons. Those one-toothed, blubber-eating fools know how to drink. They're in their natural habitat when sitting on a barstool listening to Alaskan folklore music while pounding down whisky, beer or anything with a proof label on it. Call me silly, but I can't envision Sarah Palin hanging out with this motley lot that inhabits Alaska.

How interesting would it be to watch a zebra in the wild? Aardvarks and wallabies would be boring to watch, yet the donkey show is unforgettable. They perform this act in a cage as well, but not in your typical zoo. This show takes place in a zoo named Tijuana, Mexico. Even the locals have to become intoxicated to watch this show, but where else can you have this much fun for a couple of pesos.

This is a show where the two pesos goes for the upkeep of the donkey. Mexicans believe in taking care of their animals, as do most people. Very few people eat their pets, but if somebody is hungry, who am I to say it's wrong to eat a cat or dog. I'd eat my own parakeet if it had any meat on its bones. Who could possibly dine on only tofu and lettuce? At least you can tell who practices this diet, because they look like extras from the *Night of the Living Dead*.

There are several animal-lover sites on the internet. One site had an article regarding animal hoarding. They listed three different cases in which people *hoarded animals*. Every once in awhile, we listen or read about a story in the news where an individual is reported to having too many malnourished animals on their property. All of the stories sound the same, whether the hoarder has too many horses, dogs or cats. Normally, the hoarder is an old geyser that can't even remember his or her middle name. What else are they supposed to do at their age?

We're lucky they're not hoarding their used diapers. Remember, these people are off-kilter. Whether their actions are from the results of senility or loneliness, what should we do? We should round up all the malnourished people and put them in a facility that provides food and medical treatment. I don't put animals in front of people, unless I'm betting on them to win a race or a fight.

We have too many malnourished people in this country, so why all the fuss about malnourished animals? This gives the elderly something to do and is animal hoarding widespread as some sites declare? I don't know, but I haven't seen a flock of buzzards circling the area lately, so I doubt if it's happening in my neighborhood.

If I smelled a bunch of cat urine permeating my backyard patio while I was grilling, there would be a few more dead cats. Some animal-loving site states that sometimes it costs hundreds of thousands of dollars to maintain animals taken from animal hoarder's property during trial. So why bother to take them in the first place? If they are horses, turn them into glue and if they're dogs and cats; send them to China. Why take a small problem and turn it into a larger one?

Some of these animal sites on the Internet claim that animal hoarding is similar to alcoholism. That's like comparing a cockfight to dog racing, or comparing oranges to trucks. They are two different issues altogether. Does their analogy suggest that once you hoard animals, you might as well hit the bottle or vice-versa? An article on one of these sites states animal hoarding is a community problem. So, if there is somebody that lives three streets over and has twenty-two malnourished cats running around their property, it's my problem too? I don't think so.

I can only know about a problem in my community if I see it. I helped to fight off a Walmart wanting to take roots two miles from my house, because I saw their stupid sign on the corner. However, how am I supposed to know about people hoarding animals? In this scenario, if I can't smell it or see it, it is not my problem. Besides, nudging into somebody else's business unless it has a direct impact on the person taking offense is far more dangerous.

This same animal-loving site also states, "Our laws and courts fail to provide damages that recognize the degree of injury a family has when its four-legged member has been injured or killed. In the eyes of the law, animals, even the dogs and cats we love, are nothing more than personal property." Yeah, no crap is my opinion.

I think for once that the law has it right. In case they don't know, our courts use a mathematical equation, along with other factors in deciding a reasonable judgment in a wrongful death suit for humans. If they don't, jurors would continue to give plaintiffs billions of dollars in silly lawsuits.

Not every family will receive a billion dollars in a wrongful death suit, period! Therefore, a cat or dog is worth the original cost of the animal plus a free bag of food for their next pet. Although we all love our pets, including myself, I don't expect a million dollars if some drunk ran over my cat! If the courts allowed such silly decisions as those, then people would see a dramatic increase in animal hoarding. I'd be heaving my newly stash of cats onto oncoming traffic all night long in hopes a drunk driver would hit one of them.

The American Humane Society boasts on their site that no animals were hurt or injured during the 2008 Super Bowl game commercials. Wow, I bet the directors of commercials and movies love you people! Movie making techniques has changed over the last twenty years. The filming process uses a green screen for special effects. They digitally alter the video with software, as in the commercials that aired during the Super Bowl. Does anybody think the Geico Lizard is real?

Animals can't talk, so when you saw a squirrel screaming in the roadway, was the squirrel really on the roadway, let alone screaming? Moreover, most people know that a Clydesdale horse cannot pull a train. They did not change filming techniques to suit The American Humane Society; they simply could not find a raccoon, squirrel, owl and other critters to scream on cue for the Bridgestone commercial. Either way, it's nice to know that a critter wasn't harmed, as I am constantly reminded. Holy crap, when was the last time a critter was intentionally harmed during filming under the SAG rules?

However, since this site also protects children as part of its mission statement, I found it to be more beneficial than the other sites I visited. At least there is some commonsense rationale on their stance and their mission appears to be practical, doable and manageable. Now if I can just remember where I placed my bear traps, I will pick those up as soon as possible.

Some animal groups, as in any other groups of people who only think their ideology is correct, are extremists. The types of drones that fall into their trap are the same folks who believe in conspiracy theories and spaceships. I think PETA has taken their mission statement into a completely new realm. If they think for one second, I'm going to stop fishing because they think fish feel pain, they're sorely mistaken. There is nothing better than hooking and landing a 6-10lb largemouth bass.

I caught a 10 ½ lb. largemouth bass at Blue Cypress Lake located in Florida, but it wasn't easy.

She put up a fight like a hooker who was short-changed. She dove to the bottom and struggled, but she didn't have a chance against my new 17lb-test line. Did I feel bad about the roe in her belly? The answer is no, because I ate that too. There is nothing better than soft roe from most fish. I would have only felt bad if the fish got off the hook, but I made sure she didn't by setting the hook perfectly.

She grabbed the bait, as a homeless person would grab a free loaf of bread. I reared back with all of my might and spun her head around like the girl in The Exorcist. It was a perfect catch and delicious meal. Whoever tells you largemouth bass over 5lbs. is not worth eating are people who never caught one that big. The best way to cook a fish that large is to bake it. It was flaky, tender and scrumptious.

PETA sells the silly t-shirts that say, "Eat No Animal." That's what makes America great. PETA states that these are their opinions, thus I am entitled to mine. I'm merely tired of hearing their name. I will eat chicken, beef, lamp, goat and any animals that walk, hop, slithers, swims or gallops. What is the most efficient method of pumping out nine billion chickens for the annual US consumption? We have to raise them in five weeks instead of ten to produce that many. Therefore, what is wrong with giving chickens steroids? Sports players take them all the time. The only apparent side affect thus far is death and looking like crap. If a chicken survives steroids or the debeaking process, who cares how it looks in the freezer section?

Debeaking, better known as the trimming of chickens' beaks, takes place when they are six-eight days old. Growers need to do this, because chickens are cannibalistic. They will peck each other to death. I don't see why PETA or any other group gets their knickers in a knot over this practice. I was circumcised at a very early age, but you don't hear me whining about it now. I may have screamed like a drunken Indian out of booze at the time, but as they say; time cures all things. Do you think little chickens can remember their debeaking ordeal?

If I could recall my circumcision, I would imagine I would still be screaming in pain and looking for the doctor who performed the surgery. PETA and other groups could protest doctors who perform such tortuous little snips, but their love resides in animals and their own little circumcised privates.

PETA and other offshoot groups do not believe in eating animals. That is fine to me, because I get their share. Yet, what would happen if humans stopped eating chickens altogether? Well, considering there are roughly ten billion chickens born each year in the US, it would take about two years before we could not walk or drive without hitting one. The United States would look like a giant Key West, minus Fantasy Fest. There would be enough chicken feces, so the word chicken-sh** would be meaningless. If we stopped eating cows, then the US would look like a Tijuana brothel in about six years. That's right, wherever you went, you would run into a big, brown-eyed lazy heifer.

Ted Nugent has the right idea. He hunts for his own food and keeps the population of those annoying deer from running onto our interstates. His method of keeping the venison population in proportion to nature and man is a hardy endeavor. Has anybody tried pulling a thirty-five pound tension bow? Probably not, because most of us like to buy our food already killed and ready to eat.

Ted likes to hunt, but he doesn't strike me as the type of person who's going to roast Smores around a campfire. Anybody who likes to field-dress a deer and hauls its carcass back for the rest of the post-execution duties is a true hunter. I just don't picture Ted roasting marshmallows while singing Andy Kim's, *Rock Me Gently* around a campfire.

Pigs, chickens and cows are going to suffer a little before they become a title on a menu. Does anybody think humans complain if they stub their baby toe while walking to the electric chair? According to several animal protection groups, animals have feelings. Well, has anybody seen a fish cry? Until I see one crying because I hooked him or her through an eye, then I don't believe they can emote feelings. Who could kill and eat a fish crying prior to it going in the fish batter?

Foie gras is duck or goose liver and the large retail establishment Target; was simply another target for this group. First, I would not buy foie gras from Target, let alone anything else they sell to eat. Yet, if a duck is cooked, why waste its liver? If I liked the taste of that French-crap, then I would eat it, but I can't stand it. However, some groups feel it is okay to target restaurants or even the chefs and commit illegal acts. I think these types of groups got the short-end of the stick in gray matter, because nobody has the right to put a damn duck ahead of human life, or their personal property. It's simply a damn duck. The duck is not going to cure cancer, run the country or even vacuum my house on command. Ducks do not come when you call them, nor do they know how to wash a car, no matter how hard you hit them.

Animals are also responsible for curing several medical conditions. If I hear one more story about the barbaric torture of rats or gerbils used for scientific purposes, I'm going to go off the deep edge. I don't care if they kill a million rats, as long as scientists find the cure for cancer or any other medical condition, not to mention they're ugly. It's not as though my friends and I walk around looking for rats to kill, but I'm going to snuff one if I see it around my house.

Moreover, and most importantly, I couldn't give a rat's behind on how my food is grown, let alone their living conditions. Are cows and pigs supposed to be relaxing and watching TV prior to their demise? As long as the grocery stores are stocked when I go shopping, I simply don't care. If I want steak, veal or even duck, then I expect the stores to have enough in case I'm planning a barbeque. Furthermore, if I ever see a rat or any other vermin waddling around my property, they're going to get a 9-iron up their behinds. Vermin are nothing more than plague carrying little critters and the only purpose they serve is food for other animals, such as birds of prey. If PETA members want to kiss and hug an opossum, that's their business.

Most animal protection groups do not attack individuals, but attack corporations that are behind anything they don't like or accept. Well, I have a problem with that issue, because it may put a crimp in the supply distribution.

As an example, if animal-lovers don't like the way chickens are crammed into coops, and they get their way; the price of the little peckers will go up! I like my chickens pumped with steroids or gold marigolds. The same holds true for the raising of cattle and their byproducts. I want my milk squeezed from their udders by the robotic suction cups they use now, as opposed to a gentle squeeze by human hands. I don't want nobody's grubby hands squeezing on the milk tube that may go into the next bottle of milk I buy. How do I know where that person's hands have been all day? It's bad enough about thinking about the Amish hand-churned butter, if you know what I mean.

I think we should follow PETA members with our video cameras. I have never met a member, at least none that has admitted it to me. After all, they could still be in the closet like a proud card-carrying member of the ACLU. I still have yet to meet one of those slow-thinkers. I bet you 10-1 odds, I can find a PETA member who is wolfing down a Big Mac at this very moment, while killing cockroaches in their trailer. I think PETA people eat normal food, but who really knows for sure.

At one time, animals were crash-test dummies. However, that type of abuse allegedly ended. Since we can't use prisoners who have maimed, raped or murdered people, then what's wrong with using a monkey to determine the rollover affects of a new SUV? Monkeys and chimps would work the best, because it's hard to get any other animal trained to drive a car. Besides, many nations consider monkey brains a cuisine; therefore if monkeys are not willing to participate in any crashes for the advancement of human safety, then let them be food.

If people want to wear furs, then let them! I know people who hunt, eat the critter and use their pelt. Do animal right's groups expect that same person to throw away a good mink pelt? What is the point in wasting something so valuable? If somebody kills a gator, snake or ostrich, and eats them, then nobody should mind those people wearing animal hides or skins. However, some animal groups think they know everything, so this is where their artful skills of throwing red paint on a nice new coat comes in handy. As they say, shoot first and ask questions later. I think that's a terrible mentality, because you only expect that sort of nonhuman behavior from cops and strippers.

I'm not implying that I have recipes for mink, sable, fox, or a lynx, but they're on the Internet. People should actually look it up, because most of these tweaks (animal lovers) probably couldn't even describe what a sable looks like or where it lives. With all due respect, I will give them two hints. Most sables inhabit a land where mostly rotund women harvest potatoes and drink vodka all day and the second clue is the location is not Akron, Ohio. The costs for the furs of these animals are ridiculously sky high, due to supply and demand. Does anybody realize how many sables it takes to make a long coat? Those little things only weigh about three pounds at their adult age.

A chinchilla is nothing more than a ninja-looking rat that lives in South America. They also look like they should be starring in the

Taco Bell commercials. It takes approximately one-hundred chinchillas to make a fur coat, so think of the amount of time, food and other essentials that are required to raise them. Besides, in 1829, commercial hunting began on these rodents and I am wondering what did they use to kill them? If they used a musket, the little thing would have been blow to smithereens!

Not too many people care if other people are wearing coats made from the furs of exotic animals. I contest that people who do not believe in fur coats are merely jealous. If my hardcore beliefs involved hugging animals, I bet if I won the lottery; it would cause me to change my house, let alone how I viewed animals.

The fist thing I would do is hire a Lear jet to annoy the environmentalists knowing I was leaving a carbon footprint in the sky about the size of Rosie O'Donnell's head. Naturally, I would have a limousine driver take me to my Lear jet, knowing there are enough emissions coming out of that thing to rival a Bradley tank. I would then find Ted Nugent's pad and ask if I could hunt with him.

I would want to camp in the woods, so I would pay to have Ted play some tight guitar riffs around the campfire, because I hate those frigging Smores too. Next, I would take a picture of Ted, myself, and the mortally wounded deer. I would have my venison shipped back via Federal Express, while I hopped back into a private touring bus. My bus should make it home about the same time as the Federal Express package. I would then bark orders to my newly hired chef to cook my dinner. Now, that's living my friends!

There are other things on this planet that need humanity's help and I don't believe animals make the list. How can I possibly worry about animals first, when we may run out of children in Africa at the current adoption rate? I think this is alarming and somebody needs to get involved. I know which celebrities have the most, so let's start with them. How do we know how they're treating their new off-spring? They could be beating them like redheaded stepchildren, but instead; some people only care if a stupid celebrity is wearing a dumb mink coat! Where is the logic behind that thinking, or lack thereof?

Who could write a book mentioning Animal Rights and not talk about the ASPCA? I never should have perused their website, because now I'm more confused than ever. This group began in 1866, which makes it the oldest animal-loving group in the country. Nevertheless, what kind of problems were animals having back then? The year of 1866 marked the one- year anniversary of the end of the civil war. Who was taking care of our maimed soldiers scattered throughout the war zone? Once again, when does the thinking from these groups about people come into play?

In 1866, horses were kicked with spurs and mules were beaten with a 2" x 4", so what's the big deal? There was no other way to kick-start a horse back then and mules are still one of the dumbest animals on the planet. If animal-lovers didn't mind walking over dead bodies of our US soldiers, I wonder if they tried to take action against the 1,500 or so organ grinders in New York City in the early 20th century? I guess having a monkey begging for change was a popular attraction. There was one on almost every street corner in New York by the 1920's. I think monkeys are funny, especially when they're dressed with a little hat strapped to their heads.

I definitely disagree on what age a cat should be spayed or neutered. Almost every veterinarian I contacted said between the ages of 5-6 months. I personally own two cats. One died a few months ago, so I got another that looked just like it. The sad thing is; it acts just like the one I put to sleep too. However, the thought of having your jewels removed is excruciating to say the least. I had him neutered when he was six-months old. The problem I have with most adoption centers, whether they are funded by counties or by some other local charitable groups is the fact on several occasions they would not let me adopt a little kitten until they were fixed. Each time I talked to these bucket-heads, I heard the same thing, "You cannot adopt our caged little friend, because he or she is not fixed."

I repeatedly tell these people with buckets strapped to their chins that catch their drool the same thing. I always say, "I plan on having them fixed at the proper age." On every occasion I wanted to adopt from some do-gooders, they wanted to perform these surgeries when the kittens were three-months old. That's like having a circumcision at the age of thirty. That is cruel punishment to the animal, so now I just get them from somebody's house in the classified ads. Now I understand why so many kittens receive an early dismissal from God's planet. Who wants a snaggle-toothed cat when he or she is ten years old and is already halfway through their life cycle?

I don't believe in holistic treatments for animals. What's going to be next, chicken feet and incense? This practice is anecdotal at best, so ask your dumb cat if the treatment worked on him or her and see what they say. Furthermore, why does anyone send their cat or dog to a therapist? People need to figure out the spelling of *therapist*. It can be broken down into two words, as in "The Rapist." If your puppy keeps running into walls all day, then it is probably blind or has a mental disorder. I don't think a therapist can help. In Los Angeles, they're trying to get legislation passed to mandate that pets are fixed at four months. Only in Los Angeles would they attempt such a stupid bill. The people backing this legislation should receive this treatment, not the kittens.

A tree and animal hugger is a lethal combination. The city of Huron, CA had its irrigation pumps shut off by the Federal Bureau of Reclamation because a minnow, which is on the endangered species list, is clogging the pumps. A minnow living in Fresno County is contradictory in nature. How can a little pecker survive in a farming valley? It should perish. Regardless, the valley of fertile soil is no longer. The unemployment rate is 40% and our President has not done anything to help. Thanks to Paul Rodriguez and Sean Hannity for airing a great, but sad story. My family lives in Fresno, so my dog has been in the fight and it's about time this story made it to the national level. Does our President really care?

On a final note, Bill O'Reilly nailed it again on August 18. He had a spokesperson from PETA on his show because they were protesting McDonalds. Blah, blah, blah. His interviewee was stating her discontent about McDonalds boiling chickens. Well, what about lobsters, oysters, and clams? If I had to judge the woman on O'Reilly's show, I think she's eating another brand of junk food, or at least had her share of chocolate. That's merely an assumption, because she could be big-boned. Most TV lenses add about 15 pounds, but it also depends on what type of lens they use.

O'Reilly- You went too easy on her. Although she can express her opinion, which is the greatest part of this country, I would have jumped on that situation as a fat person jumps on a McNugget when they go on sale. Keep pushing on!

The 28th Amendment would clearly define that animals are second to man and are not entitled to *special rights*. Domestic and wild animals will enjoy God's Earth, yet will always take a backseat to humans. There are current laws in place protecting animals, therefore the vocal mouthpieces can sit down in the back of the bus with their hamsters and enjoy the ride with the other backseat dwellers.

Special Interest Groups
- Illegal Aliens

Other mouthpieces on the Internet that are driving me insane are groups that are trying to protect illegal immigrants, just as much as the groups that are vocalizing their frustration about illegal Mexicans living in the US. I'm not going to fall into the trap of calling them undocumented workers, simply because the ones that I see are passed out on the corner with a bag of oranges in their hands. How hard are these people working?

According to census polls, there are approximately 8-10 million illegal Mexicans in America, of which two-million reside in California. The majority of them work in the agriculture trade and I do not see too many white people lined-up for those jobs. I've never seen an angry mob of white people, or any other ethnicity for that matter wanting to wrestle farming jobs away. The INS reports there are as many as 115,000 illegal Chinese in this country, but I don't see them picking almonds. Oh, maybe because they're busy pressing clothes and serving Wonton soup.

However, there is a problem with illegal Mexicans underbidding blue-collar jobs away from other people in the trades. I've never seen anybody roof a house faster than a Mexican, but speed and quality is not the issue. It's the fact that it does undermine US citizens having a job in the trades. It causes tension, and rightfully so.

As in any ethnicity, there are lazy, dumb and stupid people. There are also smart, hardworking and law-abiding citizens, whether they are here illegally or not. I know Mexicans that can take a cornhusk and turn it into a 3-piece Mariachi band. The people that complain about paying for illegal Mexican's health care is a pitiful argument, when according to Obama there are three times as many US citizens with no insurance

People are always telling me they wished Mexicans would stop coming into the United States. My rhetorical response is always, "why?" It's not as if many of them have an option. They live in an oppressed country and have not had a President as good as Benito Juarez, who died in 1872. Since 2004, 1,086 immigrants collapsed in the southern Arizona desert. They are risking their lives in greater numbers from the previous decade for a better place.

Since the passing of the Secure Fence Act in 2006, approximately 400 miles of actual and virtual fence are helping to seal our borders. The bill was to erect a total of 700 miles. Yet, the US can continue to build the full 1,900 miles if so desired. The sad part is that any intentional openings thus far, are only in the desert area.

The one positive thing about the wall is the fact it irked the Sierra Club, as well as a few other environmentalist groups. Are lizards and other desert critters more important than human life? A lizard can scale any wall, but maybe the turtle will have to stay in Mexico. Based on Darwin's theory of evolution, we will now have Spanish and English speaking turtles. I assume this would apply to all animals trapped by the wall.

The environmentalists are primarily concerned about the pygmy owl and the bighorn sheep. Well, if the pygmy owl can't fly higher than 13-feet, which is the claim, do we really need those things. Gee, put in some tall trees on Mexico's side and forget it. Oh yeah, they may have a tough time getting back over.

The bighorn sheep that I think they're mumbling about had a population of 1,180 in 1979, but is down to 280. Well, we're living without them, so what's the deal? Isn't it more important to address the issues of human life as opposed to animals? I'll ask Michael Vick for his opinion, because he may have something to say on this subject.

We need to seal our borders from any rag-head wearing enemy, yet the Mexicans continue to die to flee their country. I'm not going soft in my views; it's just hard to write about such a story knowing some of the facts. These are human beings, not animals. We, as a nation, no matter how powerful, can never ensure food, shelter and safety for every person in the world. If we can't accomplish this in the US, which we can't, then I rest my case.

I also hate the question posed to me why Mexicans have so many kids. Hey, when you do not have cable TV or a computer, what else are you going to do? Mexico is lacking in nightlife and leisure activities; hence, they spend their nights like teenagers in a parked car.

My wife will eventually read this book, so I will spare her the agony of reading about this hot Latina woman I met. She had me screaming things in Spanish and I never uttered a word of Spanish in my life. I recall praying to Santa Maria in a forked tongue while she was doing things …oops, here comes my wife:

The wife: "What hot Latina woman? Did you forget to tell me about this little tryst?"

Me-(Shaking like a 3-legged Chihuahua): "I was going to start typing about Governor Mark Sanford and his Argentina hottie."

The wife: "Read what you wrote moron. Now you're lying to me twice and I'm about to rip the hair out of your head. Mark Sanford's mistress has one eyebrow and looks like Mr. Ed. She is long in the face, as well as the tooth. However, I still want to discuss your Latin lover."

Me: "For the record, I never hiked the Appalachian Trail and ouch, honey, I was only kidding. Damn it, that hurt!"

The wife: "You and the dog have a bald spot, isn't that cute."

Anybody who wants to gain entrance in the US is fine, but the US needs to ensure we're not letting anybody in just because he or she has a pair of legs. I'm not making fun of our handicapped citizens, but not too many illegal Mexicans gained entrance strapped to a wheelchair. They ran, swam or walked across our porous borders. Try pushing grandma though a dessert saturated with rocks and cacti.

The rule of law must apply to everybody. The fact is we must curb the influx of illegal Mexicans or anybody else, especially since 9/11. The US has always mandated that foreigners fill out paperwork and if you are not a bonehead, you have a good chance of becoming a US citizen. Although the process can sometimes be painfully slow, it normally averages approximately one year.

I understand the division of families can be terribly painful, emotional and stressful, to say the least. There are two sides to every story and most Americans only hear the side of the story about Mexicans coming here without their entire family. Well, like I just stated, you can't wheel grandma around rocks and it is too risky for the entire family and highly uncommon for the entire family to enter illegally at one time.

You can't expect grandpa on crutches with a kid that has ADD to run for the border, because it doesn't happen that way. However, does anybody realize how many Mexicans were born in this country? So, why does the US make it so difficult for them to go back to Mexico to visit their families?

Over 500,000 illegal Mexicans left during the great depression. Some kids remained here, but others went back with their families. The kids born here can return because they are US citizens. However, our government is actually making it harder for those people (US citizens) to leave this country to visit their families than it is for illegal Mexicans to gain entrance. These are adults with passports, fought in our wars and did nothing wrong, but are not allowed back to Mexico. Our government can do this only due to the lack of record keeping, but this distrust by our government is disgusting at best.

There are pros and cons of having illegal immigrants in this country, yet the arguments should include pragmatic thinking. Otherwise, we waste our time in this ongoing angst about who should be in this country and most importantly, why. How many people have we allowed into this country for a higher education and they used that education against us?

Khalid Sheikh Mohammed, the operational planner for 9/11 attended college in North Carolina. I doubt if there's any Mexican attending a university in the US plotting any harm against us. There could be, but the US should not panic, because the student needs to stay awake in order to learn. If there are any classes after 2:00PM, forget about it.

Illegal immigrants, such as Mexicans, Chinese, Europeans, Latin America, etc. all bring something to the table. Well, I don't know what the Polish bring besides added humor. Watch one of them for a day and you'll see what I'm talking about. No ethnic jokes about Polish people materialized without any substance to support it. We definitely wouldn't be selling as much hair-removal products if it were not for the illegal Italian women that are here. That's somewhat helping our economy, so grazie!

I love the Mexican culture, their food, and zest for life. I like their passion for family unity. I like Chinese food, but I do not understand their culture and I will be damned if I can understand one word they're saying. I don't think they do either. Have you ever watched two of them speak in their native tongue? They would have a better chance of communicating by playing Pictionary.

Regardless, most people that are in the US illegally provide a service. Mexicans, as we know, work doggedly in the agricultural industry. Hispanic females work in the garment industry or hotels. How many white maids work in Las Vegas? The Chinese and other Asian citizens deal blackjack, press clothes and perform pedicures. They also ruin my commute, but I'm numb to their driving.

Illegal immigrants have very few rights, if that's what they want to call them. Their rights consist of International law, treaties and human rights. They have the right to due process, right to police protection, etc. They do not have the same rights as a US citizen. They cannot vote; however, there are a few exceptions in a couple of states that let them vote in local elections. Who cares, because most people don't even know who their tax collector is in the first place.

They cannot legally drive without a driver's license. Moreover, no state will give an illegal immigrant a driver's license. There were at least four class action lawsuits in four different states, but all four were subject to ridicule by the States' Supreme Courts. One judge got it right when he lambasted the imbeciles for attempting to turn the court into a circus event. In the argument from the plaintiff, who wished to remain anonymous, he told the judge in his argument that it was *his right* to have a driver's license. The judge had to remind Juan Doe that it is a *privilege* to drive a car and not a <u>right</u>.

Undocumented people cannot vote in the elections that count, unless they forged a document or presented a false one to obtain a voter ID card. I'm not saying all people that are here illegally are liars or cheaters, but out of the fifteen million people whom are here illegally, I'm willing to bet that 10% of them have those attributes. Therefore, it is safe to assume that 1,500,000 people who should not be voting at all, voted for Obama.

Remember, Obama promised illegal Mexicans driver licenses. Oh well, let's see if he can get our economy up and running before he starts handing out drivers licenses to people who can't read English. I hope for my safety, that all driver licenses are issued to people that can read. Naturally, we would have to adopt an exemption for those living in West Virginia.

It doesn't matter if a person running for president has testicles or had them removed, but presidents can pass very few things unless congress enacts a bill into law. Therefore, the president can promise the world, but it's not his decision to make. Look at what Clinton promised he would and did not do. He lied on both accounts, so let that be a friendly reminder to my Spanish-speaking friends.

The topic of illegal aliens was an issue for congress in the 1970's. In 1986, Ronald Regan granted amnesty to roughly four million illegal immigrants. In the same reform act, anybody caught employing an illegal citizen would receive a fine. In 2008, we had approximately fifteen-million illegal citizens. Who is watching our borders, Stevie Wonder and Ray Charles? Oh, excuse me Ray. Yet, in all reality, his sight was the same when he was alive.

We all know what President Clinton was doing while he was in office, but now we know what he wasn't doing. As the Commander in Chief, one would think that part of his job is to ensure the safety of the citizens of the United States. Perhaps that's no longer part of their responsibilities, but at least Clinton could have given us a heads-up. Thanks to him and a few other misfits working under him, no pun intended, we're dealing with a serious problem of epic proportions.

Obama recently started having every person in our local jails checked for immigration status. If they are here illegally, they are deported. However, because there is an insufficient amount of people working for the INS, they have only deported 1/3 of those individuals. If Obama ever thinks before he acts, would somebody please let me know?

However, I find this act to be somewhat cowardly and I'll explain why.

In June 2008, there were approximately 2,300,000 US citizens in state and federal prisons. One million of these inmates committed a nonviolent crime and one million committed a violent crime. In any case, these two million individuals will go back into society. There is an 11% return for nonviolent offenders and a 32% recidivism rate for the other morons. The remaining 300,000 are serving life sentences, so we don't need to worry about them. This does not include people that are on probation or parole.

Although I don't condone illegal people in this country, there are two things to remember. 1) How do we know illegal immigrants will commit another crime and 2) It would be easier to have the INS arrest illegal immigrants while they pick lettuce. The farm workers wouldn't know what hit them. While they're bent over in the hot sun picking radishes, simply pluck them like a feather.

We all seem to condone having illegal Mexicans picking our produce and changing our bed sheets, but we tend to want the other ones gone. It's a shame to have a double standard, but name one business or government that doesn't play the same game. It reminds me of a kid when you could make the rules as you go, especially if you're losing.

There will be serious problems if Obama ever unleashes the stimulus money towards construction jobs. Those jobs, which are well paying, should go to the US citizens first. It would be an egregious act to give those jobs to illegal immigrants. We all have mouths to feed and rent to pay, but US citizens are entitled to those jobs first. Yet, at the rate he's letting go of the money, there won't be a rush for jobs in a long, long, time. Damn Obama, it is not your money. Don't be so tight!

Can anyone envision the following conversation between a reporter and President Clinton regarding illegal immigrants?

Reporter: *"Mr. Clinton, are you aware there could have been as many as eight million illegal immigrants who entered our country under your watch?"*

Clinton: Pointing his finger at the camera proclaims, *"I did not have sexual relations with any Mexican woman!"*

Reporter: *"Sir, I never mentioned the words sex or woman in my question."*

Clinton: *"I'm sorry; I was thinking of something else, what did you say?"*

Reporter: *"I asked if you were aware of the amount of illegal immigrants who may have come across our border during your presidency."*

Clinton: Starting to sweat says, *"Look, hasn't every guy seen the donkey show? Tijuana is a fantastic place. I love the Mexican people. Viva La Raza!"*

Reporter: *"Never mind Mr. President, because I don't think you understood the question."*

Clinton: *"No, you asked the question and I believe the American public needs to hear the truth."*

Reporter: *"Let me rephrase the question Sir. Did you ever see the donkey show in Tijuana, Mexico?"*

Clinton: *"That is absolutely disgusting and insulting. I have never been to Tijuana, let alone partake in anything so barbaric and lecherous."*

Reporter: *"Sir, you just told me that you went to a donkey show in Tijuana."*

Clinton: *"It was not exactly Tijuana, but are you implying because I went to a donkey show, that I actually watched? Remember, I smoked marijuana, but never inhaled."*

Reporter: *"Thank you Mr. President, but I have no further questions."*

Clinton: *"Are we off the air?"*

Reporter: *"Yes Sir, we are off the air."*

Clinton: *"Damn buddy, you almost got me into some hot water with the other Mr. Clinton. Do you think I got my point across? Do you think the American people will find me credible?"*

NO SLAK as Dan Rather, *"Mr. President, my career is over and I always wanted to tell you one simple thing. You are one retarded individual."*

Tom DeWeese, founder of the American Policy Center, wrote an article in 2007 that is in complete opposition of mine. He rattled off statistics that I find incredulous and he essentially stated illegal Mexicans were a threat to the US. Yeah Tom, these are the same people flying planes into our buildings and wreaking havoc all over the US. I guess that means that US Mexicans are doing just great, but it's only the ones dying in the desert that are scumbags. Did I state your case correctly, or what did I miss?

Even though the wall between our two countries is being erected, we still have the Minutemen Militia to help save the day! Are these leftovers from 1791 when our constitution received its ratification? We don't need a stinking Militia for anything. If this group thinks they're going to protect me or anybody else from an insurgence of terrorists, I think we're all doomed.

If they're that brave, then have them strap on their muskets and head-off to the Middle East where they can actually do something worthwhile. Don't forget musket-heads, if the US wanted you to quit playing a game of Cowboy and Indians, all they would have to do is launch Tomahawk cruise missiles into your little hideout. Do you have anything to stop those? Until you do, go find another game to play, and hopefully it's one that does not involve weaponry of any type.

Arizonians passed proposition 200 in 2005. This barred social services to the fleet-footed warrior who came here illegally. In fact, any illegal immigrant involved in a car accident gets their vehicle towed as well. Cars used by illegal immigrants that cause an accident need to be confiscated, because at least the person he or she hit can have a 1972 Pinto driven by a Pollock as some sort of recompense.

Here is a list of things I would like to see changed in the US that would apply to anybody here illegally:

Read English: This is for my safety and yours. I don't care if you don't speak English. Very seldom do I run into someone asking for assistance, only to hear the response, "Que?" I expect people to read English primarily for driving reasons and me avoiding signs in Spanish. With the advent of the Internet and cable TV, most immigrants get the news in their language. As a friendly reminder, if the only sentence structure you can put together is, *I have rights*, then you will want to join the Democratic Party.

Any type of discrimination: In 2003, Oregon, which is fighting California for supreme righteousness of the liberal minded, passed a bill that stated a Fire Department crew chief must learn to speak Spanish, even though there may be only one Spanish speaking person on the crew. They started enforcing the new law in 2006. Naturally, this caused a huge uproar and the video from Fox News is still spinning around You Tube. They should fire the firefighter who can't understand English.

Perhaps that demonstrates commonsense and they don't want to buck the system. If my house is on fire, along with my three kids who look like running torches, and the Fire Captain starts rattling off in Spanish, somebody is going to be missing some teeth.

Pay your taxes: If you have a legitimate job, no matter how menial, you still must pay taxes unless you make under the poverty level, but let the IRS decide that for you.

Flag etiquette: Flying any Country's flag over the US flag is illegal and not proper flag etiquette. Anybody caught doing that should be subject to a public flogging and made to work at a Taco Bell. I don't see any Lucky Charm Leprechaun flags flown over the US flag. I can't remember what their flag looks like, but I am only assuming it has a Leprechaun or a potato on it.

Many people have come to America during its formation and started demanding things and look what happened to them. Various military leaders from France, England, Spain, Mexico and Canada tried that and they all went running back with their tails between there legs. I hope that Japan has forgiven us, but I doubt if they will ever forget the full throttling they received after they attacked Pearl Harbor.

I love Mexican food and the Mexican culture. I am merely suggesting that all Mexicans knock on our front door first. We have never denied any individual entrance, unless they were a societal screw-up from their country, or are currently traveling by camel. However, I would also ban the following:

- I would ban the sale of spray-paint to Mexicans under the age of sixty, whether they were here illegally or not. I figured at that age, it would be difficult to hold down the spray button long enough to complete various forms of artwork where it is not permitted. In case nobody told them, it is illegal to spray paint things that do not belong to them.
- All vehicles with hydraulics, fuzzy dice and painted in a gold metallic color will be confiscated and heaved into a junkyard. Naturally, only one or all three of the criteria listed above will get your car into the junkyard.

- If I eat at one more Mexican restaurant where I have to pay the Mariachi band to leave my table, then I want all of them deported as well. I am sick and tired of looking at what appears to be a remake of The Three Amigos blasting trumpets into my ear. I don't need a brass instrument blown into my left ear so loud, that blood is dripping from my right ear.

Our government allowed the US citizens to get into this predicament. We continue to turn a blind-eye, because many people in the US take advantage of the cheap labor that Mexicans are willing to work for, as well as the domination of the San Joaquin valley. Well, what did you think was going to happen? The Mexicans underbid the jobs to help rebuild New Orleans, so the black people were irate. The Mexicans are good hardworking people, but with all due respect, they can't come here illegally and start demanding things. Although that percentage of illegal immigrants that *demand things* is small, we should not condone it or accept it.

Would I give illegal immigrants amnesty? I would consider it, but not until I knew, our borders were completely sealed. Next, I would locate all the felons, people with a criminal background and ship them back to their homeland.

How many jobs can Mexicans perform that does not require English? They don't need to communicate in English as farmers, strippers, and house cleaners. Try asking a maid at your next hotel stay where a good restaurant is located. She's either going to give you another little shampoo bottle or stare at you as if you have a third-eye. However, at least they are productive citizens and working. That's the main issue and I applaud each person who is trying to make it.

It is not necessarily the cultural differences, but it is how the media portrays the typical illegal alien. Many of the stereotypes about Mexicans are simply untrue or grossly exaggerated. Yet, some of them are true, including how many are living in one apartment. You would be surprised how many people you can cram into a two-bedroom apartment if you used bunk beds that are stacked three high.

In 2006, 1,300,000 people received US citizenship. Mexicans led the pack with 173,000, but closely followed by the Chinese with 87,000 escaping their den of iniquity. Do we really need more Chinese restaurants and dry cleaners? Other ethnicities that came here were from the Philippines, India, Cuba, Columbia, Dominican, El Salvador and Vietnam. That is America, the world's only melting pot. However, the people that became citizens in 2006 did not run, swim or jump to get here. They knocked on our front doors and we opened our doors and let them enter.

Who is watching the Canadian border? Canadians can blend in with US citizens, so one would think we would do a better job protecting that border. Then again, I don't hear too many people in the US ending their sentences with, "A?" Besides, I think we can smell the French from miles away as they make there way to the border.

There are too many hate-groups on the Internet, which is only causing the pea-brains of the world to help form their opinions. Mexicans don't come here with malicious intent unless they already had those behavioral patterns when they arrived here. Most crimes committed by Mexicans already have citizenship. Yet, most people only want to report the crimes committed by those that are here illegally.

Does anybody think the Chicanos in L.A. that belong to a gang are here illegally? No, several of these people are second, third and fourth generations of Mexican descent. Crime begets crime and it is a vicious cycle, so if we want to address the crimes committed by Mexicans; then let's start by cracking down on the morons who live here legally.

From 1990 until 2008, our jail system, based on a one-day count, had a total of 4,825,000 whites, 4,664,000 blacks and 1,745,000 Hispanics. Damn, my people are embarrassing me! Well, there are more whites based on percentages...... Therefore, if somebody has the philosophy that Mexicans are sneaking across our borders to sell crack and commit crimes is preposterous. I didn't mention marijuana or cocaine, but definitely not crack. However, I doubt that many are willing to trek 75-miles through the desert to sell any weed.

I think the main discourse between the people from US and Mexico is a misunderstanding. Illegal Mexicans do not receive any special rights and taxpayers spend a lot less on them, in the way of medical insurance, than on US citizens. Most importantly, how many US citizens have hired Mexicans, whether they are here legally or not and bragged about how much they saved? We should not be a nation of hypocrites.

California passed a law stating officers cannot ask people, "What is your ethnicity or country of origin?" Who cares, because if somebody is pulled over without a driver's license, they lose their car to an impound yard. They have the right of deportation at anytime. If the I.N.S. asks for proof of citizenship, Visa or Green Card and an immigrant does not have one, then the immigrant is sometimes deported. If they don't voluntarily go, then it's up to the Federal Immigration Court.

Diversity is great, but it should never be at the cost of the American taxpayer. If I had it my way, I would have charged Elian his fair share of taxes. That inner tube kid cost taxpayers millions of dollars and turned Miami into a freak show within the first forty-eight hours of him landing ashore. Miami already has its problems, but it didn't need that disaster. Good Year should have made him a poster-boy and they both would have made millions. That is American capitalism at its finest.

President Eisenhower started the Emergency Center for Cuban Refugees in Miami in 1960. He started hauling Cubans on Freedom Flights to Miami so they could escape Castro's regime. Naturally, this irked the blacks who were living in Miami at the time, because they took most of their jobs away. *I guess some things will never change.*

Kennedy's *Migration and Western Hemisphere Refugees Assistant Act* did not make any sense, so Johnson had to throw in his two cents and amended it by implementing the *Cuban Adjustment Act* in 1966. Well, Johnson's was even worse! I love the thought of correcting something, yet making it worse and twenty-two years later; it's still in disarray.

The best way for Cubans to enter our country is in fact to swim with the dolphins, while avoiding the sharks. Once that person can prove they lived here for one year, they receive citizenship. By the end of the 1960's, over 500,000 Cubans moved to Miami and received citizenship under this act. If they make it ashore, known as *dry-foot*, they receive citizenship.

The only other way for a Cuban to receive citizenship is to move to another country first and then apply for citizenship from that country. Yet, why fill out paperwork, make phone calls, and perform all of those other nonessential duties when one can just float on an inner tube? Hey, if little Elian can make it here, then I don't see the hardship. However, don't blame the Cubans for making Miami look like a Skittle's bag that exploded. Some Italian designers created that vomit-look in the 1930's.

The whole town of Miami suffered from the same headaches that California and other states are whining about now. The teachers had to deal with Spanish-speaking children and doctors did not know how to say gonorrhea in Spanish. This caused major griping and moaning amongst the few whites and blacks that were living there at the time.

The Indians, Spaniards, French and English need to understand the US is merely a piece of property we seized so we could build Hollywood, sport stadiums, malls and strip-clubs.

All immigrants need to apply for citizenship as opposed to coming here illegally. We can no longer permit people to sneak into this country since the devastating attacks on 9/11. I am originally from the San Fernando Valley in CA and I miss true Mexican food, because it does not exist in Florida. I often think of Olvera Street and the true Mexican culture. Without sounding like a bleeding-heart liberal, my heart goes out to all immigrants trying to find a better way of life, just knock on our front door please. It is not a political comment, but one that comes from the heart.—Audios Amigos!

PS If anybody thinks they can satisfy the stomach of a hungry gringo with Mexican food, please send it. Get a hold of my agent, or you can email me at hungrygringo@Imissmexicanfood.com

The *28th Amendment* would force our broken-down congress to enact laws, yet keep them enforced. Ronald Regan granted amnesty to 4-million immigrants, but it appeared to fall apart. The INS should listen to every case on an individual basis and show compassion and not contention. After all, I wonder how many people that work for the INS were immigrants themselves. Lastly, if the Mexico City Policy changes one more time, I'm going to gag. Thanks Obama, I knew I could count on you to choke.

Corporate Greed

I recall a time in my life, when Corporate America was not as greedy as it is today. You can't turn on the TV without looking at greed in its purest form. People are trying to sell diet stuff, penis enlargement contraptions and a myriad of stuff that doesn't work. Who in their right mind would pay $1.50 for a $1.00 coin? That's another stupid show all to itself, but that's America for you! I remember when most con artists dressed like the casual Joe, but now it's people wearing suits that cause people to sleep with one eye open. Their weapons of choice to dispose of their victim include brief cases, ties, and ink.

As an example, hurricane Charley ripped my house as a good fart rips silk pants. On August 9, 2004, I hunkered in my closet as Charley and its 135 mph winds passed right over my house. My first insurance adjuster acted as though he was a hammer and I was a nail. He offered me $6,000, even though my pool enclosure alone was worth $18,000 and lying at the bottom of my pool.

I told him he was out of his mind. He kept looking at the software on his computer and told me that was the best he could offer. I asked him where he was from and he told me Kansas. I looked at him as any person would look at a deaf person when they're talking. I asked him how many pool enclosures are in Kansas. He looked at me as if I had leprosy. I knew the only thing Kansas has is wheat bugs. I told him to send out another adjuster.

After arguing with two more adjusters, over the course of three weeks, I told the last one to send out their best before I snap. A few days later, there was a knock on the door and I looked out the peephole and saw a man in a suit. I was delighted to see that Nationwide obliged me by sending their best. He said, "I'm here to help!" At that point, I realized I was doomed.

He gave me enough money to cover my garage door, pool enclosure, downed-fences and everything on my list, except the front doors. My front doors were askew and warped like a bowlegged person. He pointed to the hinges and told me that if there were three screws in the hinges, as opposed to two, the doors would not have warped. I pled my case to no avail. Nationwide never paid for my doors, but I was derelict in my duty because I knew I was talking to a suit.

It wasn't until later that I found out two screws were sufficient to meet code, but it was too late. According to Florida building codes, the installation code for exterior doors at the time was PA/TAS 201. This code means your front door should be able to withstand a 9 lb 2" X 4' shot through a canon at 35mph. I had never seen anybody shoot anything from a canon into my front doors, so what kind of code is that? Regardless, a suit screwed me and I should have known it.

Every decade, we had famous con artists, and the gullible people were their prey. Charles Ponzi was probably America's greatest con artist, but I prefer George Parker's fraudulent act. George sold the Brooklyn Bridge at least twice a week for years to unsuspecting idiots. We went from the 50's, where the most offensive word on TV was Beaver, despite the producers' claim they didn't know the meaning. The 60's was about getting stoned and the 70's was a fashion designer's nightmare. The 80's produced MC Hammer and made Michael Milken the junk bond King. It's been down hill ever since.

In the 1980's, there were approximately five people convicted of enormously sized Ponzi schemes in the world. In the 1990's, there were approximately ten and so far in the 21st century, over twenty-five. This does not include R. Allen Stanford. Stanford hired lawyers to defend his $ 8 billion Ponzi scheme allegation. I noticed some of our politicians recently started to scramble when his name became synonymous with the word *indictment*.

Aha, right when I thought the above paragraph was complete, the Grand Poo-Pa of all Ponzi schemes arose from the ashes. Bernie Madoff was sentence to 150 years in jail for bilking thousands of investors. Damn, Jeffrey Dahmer received a 957-year sentence, but he ate fifteen people. Apparently, Bernie could have eaten at least two based on simple math. Bernie made Lou Pearlman look like a poor anorexic.

I thought Lou did a great job of stiffing his friends and others out of money. However, did he do it because the cost of Jenny Craig, or was he simply greedy? This paragraph will never be complete, because the number of convicted Ponzi scheme shysters has reached twenty-nine and climbing.

These Ponzi-type schemes were large operations. The twenty-nine were people or corporations convicted of bilking hundreds of millions of dollars, or more. This list does not include the little operations, which meant they made under $80,000,000. The only good news that came out of this is the fact that I found out America is not the only country with greedy citizens. Who ever would have thought that Albania and Haiti would make the list? I would have guessed Haiti, because surely there has to be at least one obese person on that island.

It is undisputable that all Ponziesque schemes will eventually topple if they keep playing the game. These pyramid-type schemes can only stay in business for so long. After awhile, they topple down like a fat woman's breasts. The greedy people that spearhead these acts of fraud can't separate themselves from huge sums of money rolling in like the tide.

The money in these tricks act like the ocean's tide. They have a measurable ebb and flow and are just as predictable. I will never know who's greedier, a person like Ponzi, or the investor. Who in their right mind thinks there is nothing wrong with a company that is willing to pay you a 20% return on your investment? With so many people sniveling about bad investments, I think there's two suckers born every minute.

We currently have a show on TV called American Greed, so doesn't anybody else see what's happening in America? If Stevie Wonder can see what's going on, then why can't the rest of us? According to the US Department of Veterans affairs, there are approximately 500,000 homeless Vietnam Veterans. That number will double as our troops come home from Iraq and Afghanistan. The veterans of our armed forces sacrificed their lives for us. What does the United States do for them? What do you do for them? They protected my rights so I can write this book, yet the real enemy is right here in our own backyard. The enemy is greed, pure and simple.

American Greed on CNBC is about individuals or corporations who just can't get enough money. I visited CNBC's site on June 9, 2009 and typed in American Greed into their search bar. There were 1,754 video results. Wow, I can watch greedy people for hours! After watching two clips, I figured these shysters would filch Flavor Flav's gold grille for its mildew content. I shouldn't have to state the obvious that greedy people are stupid.

Greedy people, whether they are alone or working together, have a fascination of living beyond what their cranium can produce. The brain is a complex organ, yet these greedy neophytes prove some brains shrink like an unused muscle. As most of us know, the words atrophy and brain do not belong in the same sentence.

How can anybody forget about the dreadful bankruptcies of Enron, Global Crossings Adelphia and the scandal of Tyco all within a two-year period? Some of the executives from these four companies spent more money on waste, including on themselves, than all the drunken sailors in the world since the creation of the word Navy. Perhaps we could hire an auditing firm to see if my hunch is correct. After all, we would want to hire the best bean counters in the world, because that's a lot of adding.

If I'm wrong, I promise to buy a new abacus made with marbles purchased from the toy store of their choice. First, I need to find somebody that wasn't involved in some type of scandal or lawsuit: ~~Arthur Anderson, KPMG PricewaterhouseCoopers~~. Ok, Ernst and Young will have to do the job. I could use Dennis Kozlowski, the former chairman and chief executive from Tyco, because he has free time on his hands, but I need somebody trustworthy and I don't know if they allow calculators in prison.

Americans heard about the trials and tribulations of AIG, Bank of America, and hundreds of other banks who received bailout money, whether it was under the watch of Bush or Obama. Chrysler and Chevrolet asked for money and received it. In fact, Chrysler received a $1.5B bailout from the feds in 1979. The late Lee Iacocca (Oops, he's still alive) became chairman during that same year and said, "If you can find a better car, buy it!" Well Lee, it only took Americans 30 years to make their decision.

President Obama recently came to the rescue pledging that American taxpayers would foot the bill for guarantees/warranties, etc. on Chrysler products, because they just declared bankruptcy. Thanks for your support Obama! Do me a favor and take what you need out of my wallet now and kick me in my other gonad. I can't take this every other month.

Before I start writing about our current economical condition, and how we got there, I would like to thank Bing.com, Wikipedia, as well as the other trusted sources on the Internet. After spending a lot of time on the Internet, I never knew how many experts there were regarding the US economy. As most of us can attest, experts mysteriously appear after the fact, including myself.

AIG, which was one of the 350 companies who received money under the TARP program, shelled out hundreds of millions of dollars in bonuses after it collapsed. The collapse of AIG was mainly due to CDS. (Credit default swaps) A credit default swap is a non-regulated, out of control nightmare. I could get an idiot with a degree from the Wharton School of Finance and have him or her tell you what it is, but you still wouldn't understand it. I can have the same person write it in third-grade language in colored chalk, with a matching diagram, and you would still have a perplexed look. Let me take a stab at the definition, because I'm smarter than people who graduate from Wharton.

Briefly, the buyer of a credit default swap is trying to protect their bond investments in another company in case that company goes belly-up. Suppose my friend Ray-Ray wants to expand his company. He only owns one restaurant named Ray-Ray's Rib Shack, but now he wants to open three more. Instead of the bank grilling him as a lawyer does a witness, he would sell bonds to investors.

I know my friend Ray-Ray was an ex crack-head, but suppose I still buy a $1,000 bond to help him out. One day I see my friend Ray-Ray smoking crack, but there's no reason to panic! I would simply call my dipstick pals at AIG and buy a credit default. They are now acting as my big brother to help me get my money back when Ray-Ray loses everything he owns, including his teeth. The terms, which include the payment schedule and percentage, are negotiable.

Suppose we negotiated a 1% deal over the course of the contract, which would be one year. This means, I would pay AIG $1.00 and when Ray-Ray goes under in a puff of smoke, they are now obligated to pay me $800.00 assuming the bonds recover 20% on the dollar. In essence, I get my money back.

In 2007, the global bond market for CDS was hovering around the $60 trillion-dollar mark and AIG was still holding the bag for over $450 billion. As more and more companies went out of business because of the economy, AIG had to cough up $100 billion in cash. Just like Ray-Ray, they went up in smoke. We didn't have to bailout AIG, because the money they owned went to bondholders all over the world. Let them come over here and try and collect.

If the American public knew this, then everybody who owned a gun would have helped to protect our borders. We should have told all foreign bondholders wanting to collect from AIG to come here and try to collect their money, but I don't know if France could take another defeat. The American taxpayers own AIG and since it's an unregulated way of making money, then we should act unregulated. AIG took a gamble, but nobody has ever rallied around me when I lost my butt in Las Vegas. I never had a pit boss and group of blackjack dealers start a collection for my losses before I took my walk of shame.

AIG acted as though they were in Las Vegas, yet the scenario was a little different during their streak of good luck, because they still didn't know when to walk away:

- The dice shooter at the craps table was using loaded dice
- The blackjack dealers were blind and asked them what they had
- They had a blonde running the Pai Gao table
- One of them hit a royal flush on a Let it Ride table with the maximum bet
- They always found a cocktail waitress without an attitude and ample cleavage

Although the above scenario is most men's fantasy, along with a percentage of women, they could not have expected a trip like that to last forever. They took the walk of shame all right, but it was unfortunate they took the taxpayers with them. AIG is a textbook example on how to loose billions for your shareholders, yet make millions in bonuses.

The executives from AIG took the money and ran. Presumably, they attended the Michael Milken Institute of higher learning.

The executives are not near the caliber of Kenneth Lay, but I don't think anybody can reach his status in the realm of greediness. Kenneth, what say you? Kenneth, I asked you a question and I expect an answer. Oh my, I forgot, uh, Mr. Lay is busy trying to keep his butt out of hot water.

Bank of America, the country's largest bank, took billions from the feds. They took it as any fat person eats their dinner, quickly. They required an immediate cash infusion shortly after their acquisition of Merrill Lynch on January 1, 2009. Their balance sheet looked good until they bought Merrill Lynch, or at least that was the mindset of the feds.

On the other hand, there is something to note about this cry for money. I'm not a mathematician, nor an expert in the banking business, but how could Bank of America's balance sheet look good after they finished their acquisition of Countrywide in July 2008? Countrywide took a $12 billion bailout from the taxpayers in September 2007, but prior to that, they allegedly took an additional $51 billion from the Federal Home Loan Bank in Atlanta. This alleged loan is now under investigation by our illustrious Oversight Committee. Securing the loan by Countrywide is $60 billion in mortgages.

Bank of America made a bid of $4 billion for Countrywide in January 2008 after they already gave Countrywide $2 billion in August 2007 as part of a repurchase agreement. Therefore, the approximate total purchase price was $6 billion. If Countywide couldn't collect on bad mortgages, how is Bank of America? Are they going to hire Tony 4-Fingers and his brother Bobby two-toes to collect the money?

I can't keep my checkbook balanced and these clowns are dealing with numbers that have thirteen digits. Naturally, I'm including the two digits after the decimal point. It's easier for me to remember to include those two digits, because I tell strangers that I make a seven-digit salary.

The perplexing question is why Bank of America wants to purchase a company that had sleazy executives and held a boatload of foreclosures, mostly due to predatory lenders and borrowers. This looks like a *Moe bought Curly* transaction, yet Bank of America hadn't completed their purchase of Merrill Lynch yet. Bank of America announced they were going to buy Merrill Lynch in September of 2008 and the deal became complete in January 2009.

Angelo Mozilo, the former CEO of Countrywide is in *poop stew* with chunks up to his nose, yet he may walk away from this whole mess unscathed. The SEC is blaming Angelo for violating SEC rules, but I think he's holding the smoking gun. Apparently, there is a list circulating appropriately named, The Friends of Angelo.

The Friends of Angelo is a list of VIP's who received preferential treatment, such as lower interest rates, rushing mortgage requests through, refinance deals, etc. The names on this list are alarming, but I'm not shocked. Allegedly, Sen. Dodd, who is spearheading the Oversight Committee, is one of them. Along with Sen. Dodd is Sen. Conrad, a slew of congress people, a prominent judge in California and President Obama. Many of their responses are what one would think, such as; "I didn't know I was getting any favors." Yeah, and that's what Bill said about Monica too. However, I must admit that the executives at Countrywide are leading the pack in greediness, but I will let the courts decide their fate.

Next on Bank of America's radar was Merrill Lynch. Kenneth Lewis, the CEO of Bank of America, paid $50 billion dollars for a company that was losing $52MM per day between July of 2007 and July of 2008. In addition, somebody had to cough up an additional $4 billion for bonus money. Remember, Mr. Lewis had to be aware that Merrill Lynch wrote down $8.4 billion in November 2007 and another $4.9 billion in July 2008. That's like pimping out your grandmother in hopes for a higher return, because your twenty-two year old daughter came down with acne. It just doesn't make sense.

Who would purchase a company that had a reckless past? They settled more lawsuits out of court without admitting guilt than strippers that touch brass poles. Moreover, isn't it the job of Mr. Lewis to notify shareholders that Merrill Lynch was losing a lot of money and divulging their performance prior to the purchase? Alternatively, was he becoming greedy too, knowing the price of Merrill Lynch was dropping faster than a fat person eats cake?

Merrill Lynch's marketing slogan became, *Merrill Lynch is bullish on America* in 1973, but I think <u>Merrill Lynch is bullshitting somebody</u> is what people are thinking. In 1998, they paid Orange County, CA $400MM, however they didn't admit guilt. Orange County went bankrupt in 1994 and blamed part of the responsibility on Merrill Lynch. As in any lawsuit, especially of this magnitude, the plaintiff normally sues as many people as possible, hoping something will stick.

Merrill Lynch did not admit any guilt, but I wouldn't give anybody $400.00, let alone $400MM if I did nothing wrong. That's just me, but maybe Merrill Lynch was feeling philanthropic when they wrote that check. In 1994, The California Angels finished fourth in the A.L.W. and The Mighty Ducks were still in the process of trying to figure out what makes a puck slide on ice. In the same year, Disney made $400 million just on the sales of reruns of Home Improvement. At least somebody in So. Cal did something right.

In 2002, Merrill Lynch paid $100MM for publishing misleading information. At the time, CEO David Comansky publicly apologized. In 2004, there was some more apologizing when a few Merrill Lynch executives were, shall I say, slow dancing with Enron executives. Merrill Lynch cut their own deal by firing some executives and neither admitted or denied guilt.

Finally, between the years of 2007 and 2008, Merrill Lynch was involved in another mess. In this matter, a few disgruntled employees sued them. The lawsuit involved your usual suspects in any large company. The individuals included gays, different ethnic groups, etc. The EEOC has gone too far, but that's a very different subject. I wonder if there are any large companies, such as Merrill Lynch, that avoided a lawsuit by a gay person, transgender or rag-head.

Kenneth Lewis, the CEO of Bank of America, recently testified that Bank of America received emails from the feds to go through with the purchase, even though he wanted to back out of the deal. This was a shotgun wedding by some sources, but we'll have to wait the outcome from our memorable House Oversight and Government Reform Committee. For the record, our Oversight Committee is an oxymoron on all accounts. Who is spearheading the committee, New York's Governor David Paterson?

Oops! On August 3 2009, Bank of America was fined $33-million by the SEC. They quickly agreed to pay the settlement as part of an agreement with the SEC, but without admitting to the allegations. The allegations were whether they failed to disclose the $5.8-billion in bonuses paid to Merrill Lynch. Damn, right when I started to trust a suit, like Kenneth Lewis, here we go again! Thanks for proving my point that I can't trust a suit!

Merrill Lynch, Ameriquest, Wells Fargo, Lehman Brothers, Citigroup or their subsidiaries along with twenty-one other banking institutions, loaned nearly one-trillion dollars between 2005 and 2007. Several recipients of these subprime loans, better known as subhuman, had low FICO scores. (Credit rating) The word subprime did not exist until 2007, when the housing market went bust. Now, subprime ranks right up there with bling-bling in the Oxford dictionary.

Subprime loans became toxic assets to Citigroup, or any other institution. However, the CDO, (Collateralized debt obligation) helped bring Citigroup to its current position. At any rate, it doesn't matter what acronym or name the TARP recipients want to call them, they all chose to make risky decisions.

I have toxic assets myself. My garage is loaded with stuff that I can't give away on Craigslist. Therefore, the stuff in my garage is a toxic asset. I paid for something that I can't give away. Aha, maybe I should ask for some of that stimulus money.

It doesn't take a brain surgeon to determine that you can only make so many loans to dead beats, before you become bankrupt. It doesn't matter if you use the FICO or the newly created, yet not well-liked Vantage score. Where did these lending institutions go wrong in lending people money to buy homes?

I was born in a house built in 1960 and I have the original loan application. It consisted of a single sheet of paper that listed my parent's assets and their debts. Today, most lenders use a debt to income ratio, which is like loaning a heroin addict a spoon and expecting to get it back.

The debt to income ratio determines if the applicant can pay back the agreed upon monthly payment, plus make essential payments, such as utilities and other essentials to live. Well, chances are they can, otherwise they wouldn't receive a loan. Yet, doesn't anybody think the little worm isn't going to take a vacation or buy a new surround sound system?

Lenders made too many loans to people with FICO scores that were low enough to get them into an A.R.M. (Adjustable Rate Mortgage) Several articles were written to suggest that as many as 60% of the people who bought their first house between 2003-2005 used an A.R.M., even though they could have purchased it using a conventional mortgage.

The dolts that borrowed on an ARM in 2005 and lost their house used a two-year ARM. The people that lost their houses in 2009 were the dummies that used a 4-year ARM. Wait until 2010 when the 5-year ARM's cause those morons to become upside down. The year 2010 will not be a pretty picture in the housing industry.

The Clintonesque idea of having everybody living the American dream became a nightmare. As people continued to buy homes, just as many were taking out second mortgages to help pay credit card debt, or take a trip to the Bahamas. As people continued to spend like crazy, the feds had no choice but to raise interest rates to undercut inflation. Unbelievably, when the majority of people are spending money, inflation is on the horizon.

Another group of greedy imbeciles was the people that watched *Flip This House* too many times. I know several people who bragged about how many houses they bought in a month and the next thing I knew, they were living in a cockroach-infested apartment. Naturally, this is after they sold their luxurious cars as well. I guess we can call these people opportunists, as opposed to greedy, but they weren't that bright.

When the feds became giddy about inflation, they had to raise the interest rates. In 2006, there were several warnings by people around the world about what would happen in the years to come regarding the housing crisis.

There was an article written by Dudley Baker and Lorimer Wilson that warned us of the impending doom and gloom. According to their terse narrative on the foreclosure market, they noted that foreclosures were up by 13% in December 2005, but rose to 27% in January 2006. Furthermore, the amount of foreclosures was up by 45% from

January 2005. Did that stop people from buying homes? The answer is a resounding, no!

Although home sales started to plummet, so did the rest of the economy. When people start to lose their homes, there's less cash traveling from register to register. When companies start to tighten their belts, it normally leads to layoffs. When layoffs happen, more people lose their houses. Most importantly, the D.J.I .and other global markets simultaneously drop in value faster than Ed McMahon goes down a flight of stairs.

There was a lot of greed on both sides. Clearly, there were greedy institutions making risky decisions, and don't forget about the short-bus riders who purchased at the wrong time, or spent their refinance money foolishly. People were taking seconds out on their houses to buy plasma TV's, stereos, iPods, iPhones, stainless-steel barbeques, and cute little waterfalls for inside their homes. Executives of the lending institutions, along with the recipients, all had a dream, but I'm sure the crocodile hunter did too.

A newly created term called predatory lending is easily disputable. Although there were fraudulent acts conducted by mortgage brokers, I surmise to say there were more predatory borrowers. Caveat Emptor is a widely used term. This Latin term simply means, *let the buyer beware.* Therefore, when you buy a used car from a man named Billy-Bob and the carpet smells of mildew, wouldn't you become suspicious that it was involved in a flood? On the other hand, do you believe Billy-Bob when he tells you it's wet because Frank the mechanic was working on the inside of it and he sweats too much? More than likely, a judge will utter these famous words to you when you try to get your money back after you purchased your swamp-filled wreck.

I do not feel sorry for people who did not ask any questions, but simply signed mortgage documents. If they did not know that interest, PMI, and other components of a mortgage transaction are negotiable, that's not my problem. In addition, I do not feel sorry for people that did not know what an A.R.M. could do to them. In this case, the long arm came out and slapped the crap out of them.

Several borrowers, as noted in an article in the New York Times on January 17, 2008 simply lied about their annual income. Some creative geniuses altered their paycheck stubs by using $30.00 software. As a result, the people that lied about their ability to make the payments, were five times likely to default and go into foreclosure. Therefore, I would like to thank those shameless people for my inability to buy houses that are currently in foreclosure. The banks are clinging onto them as a slow kid does his chinstrap.

People are only fascinated with CEO's bonuses and salaries during the bad times. When everything is running smoothly, nobody says a word. It's only when there's a lackluster performance in the company's revenue, due to an economical downturn, that people start sniveling. Watchdog groups sprouted-up on the internet like mushrooms reporting CEO's compensation. In fact, the AFL-CIO has their 2009 Executive Pay Watch! In my opinion, this is another worthless endeavor heaped onto their mission statement.

Countrywide's former CEO, Angelo Mozilo, received enormous bonuses, but nobody brought it to the forefront until June of 2009. He is one of the hundreds of executives who took a huge bonus on the way out the door. Merrill Lynch executives took a whopping amount in bonus money also.

Nevertheless, there are just as many CEO's not in the banking world that voluntarily took pay cuts and cited zero bonus money for 2009. I applaud the CEO's who lead by example. There is too much media coverage on the shysters who took bonus money for letting their companies fall into the abyss, as opposed to upstanding leaders who took the right course of action. After all, how many millions can one spend?

I challenge Robert Iger, Thomas Ryan, John Donahoe and David Brandon to curb their bonus money. The respective leaders from Disney, CVS, eBay and Domino's Pizza should watch their compensation. I understand the notion that the frontline employees keep their operations running and they don't answer to them. These CEO's must answer to Wall Street and their investors.

When each of these gentlemen looks in the mirror each morning, do they see a greedy person, in the sense that if they curbed their compensation, they might have saved a job in their organization? I've often wondered what CEO's think about in tough economical challenges. If a CEO wants to maintain his job, he or she must answer to shareholders or a nagging spouse. Damn, what do you do? I think I just answered my own question. I would slash jobs like Jack the Ripper, yet wear an eye-patch over the one eye that does not shut at night.

Most large organizations can afford to keep good employees and weather the storm without laying them off. Conversely, when companies announce a layoff, it's the perfect time to get rid of any driftwood that's been wandering around their organization as though they were searching for the Loch Ness Monster during their tenure.

If Bill Gates found out how much Michael Dell and Steve Jobs made in bonus money in 2008, he may want his old job back. How can Bill manage to live on a poultry million dollars a year? Bill, if you need financial advice, I'll give you some. My advice is to ask me and not Merrill Lynch. I can get you a job in motivational speaking or something comparable. Better yet, how about if you start your own TV reality show aptly titled, Chillin' with Bill.

It would beat anything else on NBC. NBC's ratings are so bad; they would probably lose to themselves. Yet, if you aired Chillin' with Bill, you can also write it off on your taxes as charity work. In addition, this would tip the scales in your favor to win the Albert Schweitzer award. If you need anything else, drop me a line.

I just love Dell computers with XP software. Vista is fantastic software, but it needs work, like an undeveloped girl. I also love Mac computers, but I can't afford one. I'm in a quandary, because if this book doesn't sell, I may have to go back to work as a lumberjack living in a trailer on the outskirts of a small desolate town. Although I can barely afford it, I'm going to send each one of these three pioneers an autographed copy of my book.

I hope they will see me as a thought provoking, yet gentle young man with philanthropic views. I have ideas on how to gel the world into peace and harmony, however I need a good working computer to help pull that bulls*** off. In fact, a new computer will allow me to peruse the Internet at faster speeds, thus allowing me to keep up with the research required to zap those annoying mosquitoes in Africa. Please help gents and thanks for the kind words in advance.

After spending countless of hours on research, I have reached my conclusion on what happened and that is simply nothing! The CEO's who put their companies in the drink claim they didn't do anything wrong, including taking bonuses out the door. The supposed predatory lenders claim they did nothing wrong, just like the predatory borrowers. Everybody involved is pointing to the other person or group, but neither one is taking ownership. Therefore, we don't have a problem. If we don't have a problem, then take the $800 billion and divide it evenly to the 135 million taxpayers. There, problem solved! Each taxpayer should receive their stimulus check of roughly $6,000 as soon as I submit my report to the President.

In this case, *the 28th Amendment* would contain a clause that anybody caught cheating, lying, or knowingly screwing the public for their personal gain would have to perform community service. Well, the perfect solution is to have these liars and cheaters push our trains. This would eliminate a lot of carbon going into the sky. It would be funny to see suits pushing a train. Moreover, because these crimes are so egregious to the rest of the hardworking community, they first must spend five years in a state prison holding onto a colored scarf belonging to either, Jerome, Ray-Ray or any incarcerated rapper, while wearing *I hate Rap* t-shirts.

Going Green, or going with the flow?

In doing research for this book, I don't think I visited a website where corporations didn't proclaim they were *going green*. Without reservation, I visited thousands of sites and I think the only ones that did not mention anything about going green were some of the sites promoting fat people. I can see why some of them chose not to promote going green, because they have never seen the color, let alone eaten it.

Google advertises heavily on their site on what things their organization is doing to go green, but I can't find anywhere through their search engine who coined the phrase. I find that amusing. Everybody is going green, but nobody can trace who started the dumb saying. I'm surprised Al Gore didn't take the credit in his book about global warming. Wait until he reads this part of the book, because his face will be plastered all over Google after somebody types, "Who coined the phrase going green" into their search bar.

Fortunately, our collapsing economy has caused several people who believe in global warming to become silent. The people whining about global warming are now whining about unemployment or their imminent foreclosure. It's actually been somewhat quiet on the *going green* front. Michael Jackson's demise caused the media to talk about him for an extended period of time. Therefore, I want to thank Michael for his contribution to get the media to think about something else, besides going green.

I have noticed that over the years, more celebrities are joining the cause in their feeble attempt to protect others and me from the polar caps melting, thus washing my body out to sea. Celebrities tend to bend to the left in their political convictions; therefore, I believe it is strictly peer pressure. How many Republican celebrities are there? They must be in the closet, like the other sordid lot that calls Hollywood home.

I don't need a motley group warning me about their estimates on when Earth will succumb to a cataclysmic event due to environmental changes. It's hard enough to dodge hurricanes, earthquakes, fires, floods or a car salesman.

Within reason, it's safe to assume our planet is at least hundreds of millions of years old. Nobody knows with certainty, but I have my own theory on its age. If Strom Thurmond and King Tut's skeleton looked the same before Strom's departure, then Dr. Boltwood's formula for radiometric measuring is flawed. I decided to investigate my claim and in five minutes, I realized the decay constant in his formula has to be divided into itself, as opposed into the number one.

That makes Earth 500 million years old. For the last 60 years, scientists thought Earth was 4.5 billion years old and I figured it out in five minutes. It's a simple mathematical mistake, like not carrying a one when multiplying. Oh well, start rewriting the history books and please quit trying to establish a birthday for a rock!

Where is the scientific data to support global weather change? Better yet, how long has this data been collected? There is insufficient data. How can my local weatherman blow his forecast the next day, yet believers in this hoax believe in predictions taking place in decades? Moreover, are scientists infallible? They have proved themselves wrong on several occasions. Doctors, scientists, and even plumbers are not always right.

The Organ Institute of Science and Medicine has over 39,000 signatures on a petition that states there is no foreseeable catastrophic doomsday. Oh, and these are people with PhD's and a tad smarter than the motley group pushing us in the going green direction. We have over 14, 15-million people unemployed in the US as I write this paragraph and it is only getting worse. During this time of social upheaval, we do not need a Commander in Chief who keeps talking about clean coal.

Coal is black, dirty, and nasty, but our President seems hell-bent on making this his top priority, along with his socialized medicine program. Perhaps our President should ask the 10-million US children who go to bed hungry every night. Although fat children should go to bed hungry more often, we should still care.

I'm not a scientist, but I know C02 stimulates plant growth. I know C02 is required for photosynthesis, so when did carbon dioxide become bad words. It's as though every time somebody says carbon dioxide, they might as well be saying Adolph Hitler. Since when did cow farting become a threat? Humans also produce methane and there are roughly six times more people than cows on this planet. In fact, when humans fart, there is also an emission of CO2. Notwithstanding, I've emitted far more destructive toxins after a night of beer drinking commingled with Taco Bell. Their slogan of run for the boarder creeps into the minds of my unfortunate victims.

Scientists believe that ruminants such as cows, sheep, camels, water buffalos, and other cud-chewing critters produce 90% of the methane gas. However, if there are only two-billion cows and six-billion people, I would do another survey. The most important part of this scientific data collecting is to ask volunteers not to eat eggs, cabbage or sauerkraut before they blast one off.

We're all waiting in anticipation for an event that will more than likely not happen, but sit idly by as millions of people across the globe go to bed hungry every night and live in third-world conditions. They have no running water, electricity or shelter. I need to stop, because I'm having flashbacks of Akron, Ohio.

One would think our far-left lunatic fringe would want to help eradicate those unnecessary atrocities, because it's something we can fix now. We have food, medicines, and several vacant houses in the US. As opposed to putting people who live in huts in our empty houses, the left-wing nuts are helping to enact laws as to what type or how much energy we can use in the houses we own.

Waiting for a nonevent to happen is like watching Al Gore speaking about this sordid subject. It is boring, nauseating, and plain ridiculous. With all due respect, Al *took the initiative to create the Internet.* He certainly had the time, because his boss was too busy handling a blue dress and a cigar.

Celebrities and their far-left ideologies is nothing new. They jump on any bandwagon as a fat person jumps on cheesecake. Are these people ever going to snap out of it? They're entitled to believe in what they want, but I appreciate people who practice what they preach.

Most celebrities have multiple homes, cars, and fly more often than the average working class stiff. When they work, do you think they're acting under LED lights, or using lamps that are thousands of watts? That's if they're working inside, but if they're shooting something outside the studio, sets require generators. Common generators that you see are 1,400 amps. It is enough amps to power a small city.

If celebrities travel to a foreign place, such as North Carolina to make a movie, do you think they fly or ride their bikes? Moreover, when common folk stay at a hotel, they stay at reasonably priced places, better known as dives or motels, whereas celebrities stay in hotels.

The obvious distinction between the two is lighting. When someone drives into a motel parking lot, it appears that the parking illumination is coming from a candle. Once the skeleton key unlocks the tarnished doorknob, there is normally only one light switch. This switch controls the single lamp in your room. Most of these dumps don't have a restaurant, spa, exercise room, etc. The only thing that is going to give you a message is the bed lice.

Conversely, when somebody drives into a nice hotel parking lot, the lighting resembles Main Street at Disneyland. After you swipe your room key to unlock the door, the occupant will notice more than one switch and lamp. In addition, there are restaurants, a light in the pool, an exercise room that is open all night and the maids do not have an attitude. How many celebrities are hitting a switch in a Budget 8?

Furthermore, many of them are driven to their hotel after a day's shoot, but it's not in a Prius. After all, how can a celebrity look important and maintain their attitude if a man named Winston chauffeured them to their hotel room in a Prius? A Prius with tint would look hideous. Notwithstanding, but putting tint on a Prius is waste of good tint. Michael Eisner claimed he owned a Prius, but I've seen him in the back of a limousine plenty of times.

There are groups and authors that concocted a formula to determine how much of a *carbon footprint* an individual emits. One of their examples is comparing how much carbon dioxide a car, train or plane produces. To determine the emissions for an individual, you divide how many passengers are in the aforementioned vehicle. This covers the butts of rich people who spew global warming out of their mouths. Does it really matter if the plane is full or not? It doesn't matter if the plane was full or had one passenger. The bottom line remains the same. It still produces approximately twice as much carbon dioxide than a car.

In the July 2009 edition of Popular Science magazine, the cover caught my attention as a smorgasbord does a fat person. It caused me to jerk my head around like slow people when they see a camera flash. I spotted the perfect article for this chapter on the cover. It stated, The Future of the Energy Power Plan. There was a not a chance I was going to keep walking without buying it. I would associate the same feeling if I were cruising Las Vegas Blvd. with $20 in my pocket.

Solar Power- Although I can never get a solar light to work in my yard, maybe these guys had an idea. In a city north of Los Angeles, there are 24,000 mirrors planted on twenty acres. The concept is to have the mirrors reflect the sunlight onto water filled boilers. Great concept, but I don't want to fly over that area. I wonder how many one-eyed pilots we'll have in ten years.

Hydroelectric- It has always worked ala Hoover Dam. It's reliable and efficient, yet the environmentalists think they're harming the fish. Somebody needs to take these guys fishing in Lake Mead. I think that lake has the largest striped bass west of the Rockies. Every time I've fished there, I've never struck out and I never reeled in a one-eyed fish.

Biofuels- When I hear of any progress, I'll let you know.

Wind Power- These things need wind to work, right?

Nuclear Reactors- What's wrong with reactors? Can anybody recall when the last time a US nuclear aircraft carrier or submarine simply blew up? This is an open and shut case, because there is no sane argument not to build reactors. Most people associate these with Chernobyl and nobody wants one in their backyard. There are reactors in thirty-one states. I know people are concerned about the waste. My argument is that the Cuyahoga River is still running, so put the goop in there.

Geothermal- If this doesn't cause Iceland to melt, nothing will. This concept of producing energy is silly and not even worth mentioning. I'm open to new ideas, but at one point, one has to stand back and say, "What was I thinking?"

My dad made me read Popular Science when I was a teenager, along with three other magazines he received in the mail. They consisted of National Geographic, Popular Mechanics, and Life. This is the only one I've ever purchased myself, but the ads got my attention more so than the article about future power options. In the back of the magazine, there were at least five different ads for improving your sex life or making your penis larger. Do the ads insinuate that most of their readers have problems in that area? We called lab jockeys nerds when I was going to college. I guess some things never change, because those poor little guys are still looking for love.

In the past, John Travolta gave his dissertation on global warming and claimed we should do something about it. Well, I have an idea for you Vincent Barbarino! Why don't you stop flying? If I'm not mistaken, jets emit carbon dioxide, kind of like car exhaust, except twice as much. Since you're one of the global warming believers, then sell your squadron of planes. I think you have more planes than Chad's military.

It's only a matter of time before the French take another beating. As you know John, they're still fighting in Operation Epervier in Chad. Therefore, when the thugs shoot down their Mirage jets, perhaps you could loan those whine-guzzling buffoons a couple of your planes. However, you would be doing them a service if you had some ultra-lights.

If a person flies more than two times a month, they should be automatically disqualified from talking about global warming, period! If John claims he travels all over the world to preach about global warming, then that's acceptable.... Yeah, okay.

PS John- I am deeply sympathetic to the loss of your child, for I could never understand how that feels. Keep up the good work and contact me. I recently moved, but you can find me on the Internet.

Elizabeth Hurley claims she recycles her old clothes. Good for you cupcake, can you send them to me please? I promise to put them to good use. Contact John Travolta for my address. Surely, he found it by now. Remember, I will also take any old jewelry, cars, houses, etc. I surely want to do my part to recycle. This noble endeavor leaves me breathless and intoxicated. Wait, I'm thinking about your clothes, my bad.

In 2005, Governor Arnold Schwarzenegger stated that global warming is *an indisputable threat.* Yet, he continues to commute to Sacramento several times a week by private jet. I can understand why he does not want to live in Sacramento, but I think that's hypocritical.

Reportedly, his home in Brentwood, CA is 6,000 SQF, complete with pool. It's hard to tell from the aerial view of his home, but I thought I saw solar panels and windmills to generate electricity. This would offset his carbon footprint that he leaves in the air. If global warming were an indisputable threat, then why would he risk a possible early termination of our icebergs by flying all the time?

Arnold, would you send me an autographed picture please? I want a picture of you from Kindergarten Cop. I think that was your best role. The Academy overlooked another great movie.

PS Send it via Fed-Ex, so I can get carbon residue on my hand, which would make the whole experience hilarious. Thanks in advance and good luck with your State's deficit.

In my humble little opinion, I think Tom Cruise is a wing nut, so whatever he thinks about the environment; I do not care. I don't think anybody knows for sure how many planes, motorcycles, or cars Tom owns, let alone how often he uses them. Besides, if I start talking about Tom, I'm going to snap and start whining about Scientology. I have premonitions that Ron Hubbard will arise from his deep sleep, board his spaceship and sue me.

I don't know how Paul McCartney thinks, but according the UK's Food Climate Research Network, livestock is responsible for 15% of the greenhouse gas, methane. Therefore, Sir Paul started a campaign called Meatless Mondays. Damn, that's my porterhouse night and I am not going to stop. Notwithstanding, I don't live on that little island, so I don't think the same statistics apply in the US.

That's what animals do Sir, they fart and crap. If we stop eating beef, then PETA would really be annoyed when I start running over cows because they're on the highway. Reports indicate that another 15% of GHG's are involved with food production. Does that mean we should stop eating altogether? The article I read on Green Living Ideas site said, "Scientists, chefs and celebrities are supporting McCartney's

Meatless Mondays campaign." I wonder why they didn't use the words *normal people*.

Moreover, I bet not every chef of a steakhouse is participating. If Paul still owns a few homes in the US, does he swim or take a sailboat to get here? Seriously, the backstroke is great exercise and there's not a more tranquil way of traveling than by sailboat. It's peaceful, serene and doesn't leave a carbon footprint.

Whenever I fly across the pond to visit the Queen and her delightful brood, I hire a private 747. Following aside my carbon-producer are two smaller planes so they can spell N.O. SLAK in the air as I'm cruising. I'm not bashful about my mode of transportation. I only use one orifice to speak and not from both, as many celebrities tend to do.

I'm not giving up my seventeen mansions and I don't care how much energy I'm wasting. I leave all the lights on just to annoy any environmentalists who try to fly in and out of the US like a stealth bomber. If all of my mansions were next to each other, the lights would rival Manhattan at midnight on a clear evening from only 2,000 feet above the ground.

In 2007, Jennifer Aniston revealed that she brushes her teeth while showering. She further stated that a three-minute shower is equivalent to what an average African would use in water during an entire day. Jen, Jen, Jen.

Let me say that according to dentists, it takes approximately two minutes to brush your teeth properly. Therefore, you're only allowing yourself one minute to clean your body and whatever else you do in the shower. I find that sort of nasty. I carefully chose the word *sort*, because I'm a healthy male.

As I stated, I don't know what you do in the shower, but unless you have two other arms that we don't know about, I have to wonder. Well, thanks for thinking of the Africans and getting the brush-wash technique fashionable.

I tried your technique, but my showers lasted sixteen minutes and I didn't like the buildup of toothpaste on my tile. I went back to brushing my teeth over the sink. Keep me posted on any new techniques you discover in the shower, because I would love to hear all of them, trust me.

People who believe in going green refer to others who don't believe in their theory as *brown*. I think this is a racial remark against our Hispanic population. Wait until my maid finds out, because she will get involved and put an end to this term. If anybody has witnessed an irate Latina woman, then I would stop using this term immediately. In addition, my maid does not go anywhere without her dynamite laden donkey.

I never heard anything about Celine Dion going green, yet the do-gooders attacked her over an alleged water bill from 2007. Apparently, she used 6.5MM gallons of water during the construction on her new crib in Florida. I can equate this type of water usage to flushing a normal toilet 6,000 times a day.

If I had her money, I would make her new house my maid's quarters. Welcome to Florida Celine and when you get a chance, stop by so you can sing for me. Keep up the good work. In case you actually want to croon my night away, please see John Travolta or Elizabeth Hurley for my address. Wear something conservative, because I'm married, but please don't tell Elizabeth in case she sends her clothes.

The guitarist for U2, better known as The Edge, has Malibu's knickers in a knot. He purchased over 120 acres in the Santa Monica Mountains for a reported $15-million. Although he claims his new house will be environmentally friendly, other people disagree. His opponents made comments such as, "Does anybody realize how much energy and water will be used? In addition, how much carbon dioxide will be emitted from the trucks used to transport the building materials?" I don't condone violence, but if that comment doesn't facilitate a slap to the chops, nothing will.

If I had The Edge's money, I would buy him and U2. How can the residents of Gomorrah's twin city get upset about a little carbon dioxide when The Edge simply wants to build a new house? Is Malibu's soil the landing for the second coming of Christ? I'm not a theologian, but I doubt if Mel Gibson's house is the landing zone for Christ's return, let alone something he's passionate to see.

Malibu has wildfires, mudslides and egomaniacs, all of which are out of control. The gumption of the going green group to whine about another house built in the canyon overlooking the ocean is utterly ludicrous. Do these environmental neophytes think shovels and mules built the existing houses?

The Edge claims he is going to install solar panels to generate electricity for his grandiose mansion. Who wants a mansion with solar panels on top of their roof? That's similar to wearing a plaid suit to a wedding; you simply don't do it. It's like putting suntan lotion on an albino. Besides, you cannot hurt that den of iniquity. My advice to The Edge is the following:

   a) Build the most obnoxious mansion in Malibu and let everybody know there's a new sheriff in town. In fact, put a sign on top of your roof that states, "These are not solar panels yanks!"

   b) I would also build a telescope bigger than the one at the Griffith Park Observatory.

      Do you know how much you can charge people for snooping in the houses of the celebrity underworld? Wow, you would be richer than you are now.

Keep on rockin' Edge and thanks for giving so much to the victims of Katrina. I'll never like boiled potatoes, lamb and warm beer, but if you and your mates want to jam at my house, give me a call. I can get you and the band into Walt Disney World free, so it may be worth the airfare to Orlando.

The same group labeled Simon Cowell as brown. That's because he's filthy rich. If I had his money, I would buy the whole gang from American Idol. I would buy Simon, just so I can prove to my friends that I found a Brit with all of their teeth. I would buy Paula Abdul to be my maid and Randy Jackson as my butler. I didn't forget Ryan Seacrest. He would work hand-in-hand with Randy. After Randy answers my phone or door, Ryan would announce who requires my attention.

I cannot have my guests listening to Randy saying, "Yo, what's up dog?" My friends consist of dignitaries, scientists, scholars, experts, female gymnasts, doctors and war veterans. They would not understand

Randy's urban slang. Most importantly, if one of my Vietnam friends heard that annoying greeting, they may snap.

What did Simon ever do wrong? It isn't his mission statement to help save the planet, so why is he targeted? Apparently, successful celebrities are *brown*, if they choose not to believe in this silly global warming. His main job on American Idol, besides the obvious, is to keep the ratings up. He knows it, his agent knows it and I know it. An inbred hillbilly knows it too.

If it wasn't for his witty sarcasm and brutal honesty, I don't think the American version of Idol would survive. Simon is not splitting the atom or doing anything that requires a doctorate degree, but he's memorable, to say the least. Moreover, in Hollywood, that's a requirement.

PS Simon, would you please ask Paula to send me a signed photo of her from the 80's, because she was hot! Oh Paula, you know I'm only joking doll-face. When you get time cupcake, will you email me back? I emailed you under the name *cold-hearted snake* this time. I heard you left the show, but Simon can rollover and hand you a copy.

The 28th Amendment would require anybody who uses the phrase *going green* to put a cork in their other orifice. The cork-holders would easily be distinguishable from others and they would help to keep our planet methane free.

A letter to our President

Obama recently completed his first year in office and all I can see from my trailer is my gasping dog with nothing to eat. Obama is pushing his socialized medicine plan down our throats, as opposed to nourishment. As he mounts his daily pulpit each day to preach his knowledge on geothermal, I kneel to my porcelain God to heave and pray.

(RSV Exodus 20:3-6).
You shall have no other gods before me. You shall not make for yourself a graven image, or any likeness of anything that is in heaven above, or that is in the earth beneath, or that is in the water under the earth; you shall not bow down to them or serve them; for I the Lord your God am a jealous God, visiting the iniquity of the fathers upon the children to the third and the fourth generation of those who hate me, but showing steadfast love to thousands of those who love me and keep my commandments.

I stated the scripture above, because as I wrote porcelain God, a lightning bolt whizzed by my scalp. However, how am I supposed to react when I see our country going down in a burning ring of fire? For Pete's sake, another lightning bolt! What is going on here? Wait, what am I thinking? It's Florida in the summertime! That explains it.

Obviously, our good Lord has a sense of humor, because look what He has created. We have a cast similar to the Three Stooges running the USA and it's as embarrassing as having insufficient change for a prostitute on nickel-night.

Obama, Biden and Pelosi make The Three Stooges look like Rhodes Scholars. The fourth in line is Senator Byrd from West Virginia, but he's only a threat to himself. Surely, it has to be downhill after ninety-something. I do not picture him arising every morning to hike the

Appalachian Trail, but if he were given the strength, I'm sure he would run into Governor Mark Sanford. Together, they could tag-team any Argentina beauty. Wait, does the Senator have any blue-pills and an oxygen bottle?

Dear Mr. President,

With all due respect, what are you doing? Are you ignoring the will of the people? As you know, your Obama-Care has stirred the nation. We, as a whole, do not want it. Your approval ratings are in the drink and fifteen million people are unemployed. You can no longer blame this on the Bush administration. You have managed to find a way to make Bush look heroic, articulate and smart. Remember, Bush could not enunciate the word "subliminal."

Chronologically, this is what I know about you and after you read this, you may discover some things you didn't know about yourself.

Reverend Jeremiah Wright was your Reverend for twenty years, but you claim you never heard him say anything construed as anti-American. In fact, when some of the Reverend's tapes aired on TV, you started tap dancing like Sammy Davis, Jr. Why did you distance yourself from him suddenly? I thought he baptized your children, as well as performed your wedding ceremony. Did the press get that wrong?

I did not pick Catholicism, but I was in no shape to pick any religion. I just came out of my circumcision coma and some man dressed in black was splashing water on my face. I left the church when I was fifteen, because I could never understand a spoken word. They spoke mostly in Latin during those years.

Reverend Wright, despite his gravelly voice, is understandable. However, you still claim you never heard him say anything anti-American or racial. I can guarantee you that Father Nash from my church never said anything anti-American or anti-black. If he did, then he said it in Latin and I have an excuse. What is yours?

William Ayres was at your house while you ran for Senator. How could you possibly let a scumbag like that in your house? Charles Manson ate dinner at a Denny's three miles from my house, as the Tate-LaBianca murders took place. If I knew Charlie was there, should I have invited him to break-bread with me? As we all know, Denny's is not a 5-star joint and Charlie never physically killed anybody, right? You knew William Ayres and you knew what he did. That is inexcusable, or did you want bragging rights of keeping company with white trash.

While you were campaigning for office in Oregon, you said, "Over the last fifteen months, we've traveled to every corner of the United

States. I've now been in 57 states. I think one left to go. Alaska and Hawaii, I was not allowed to go to even though I really wanted to visit, but my staff would not justify it." Dude, er, Mr. President, how many states do you think you oversee? Later on that day, according to an article in the Los Angles times, you said 57 states again and were cut-off by one of your staffers. Mr. President, you said 57 states twice! Do you know how many states came with the job? Are you smarter than a 5th grader? Hold on, it gets better Sir.

For somebody who claims he is smart, how could you pick Joseph Biden as a running mate? Was he the only one left with a pulse in the Democratic Party? Biden is a gaffe-machine! Before you officially took the oath into office, he tried one of his funny jokes and it went over like a bomb on Hiroshima. You gave him a look as if you wanted to slap him right there on the spot. Well, the difference between you and I is the fact I would have done it.

Speaking of the gaffe-machine, have you seen him lately? The last time I saw him, he was swigging down a girly beer on the White House lawn with you, the cop and the professor. Wow, that must have been a real round-table discussion. I would have been bored before I took my first swallow. If you added an Indian to the mix, the press may have confused you folks for the Village People.

You picked Joseph Biden as your running mate knowing that the witch from the West is the third in command. God forbid, but if something were to happen to you, we are doomed. Now I see why the President and Vice President never travel together.

In March of 2009, Hugo Chavez, the little feller from Venezuela, called you an ignoramus, which was after he called President Bush the devil. However, you chose to meet him the following month. There you were, in all your glory, shaking hands with the pint-sized dictator. Cameras caught you laughing and joking with this clown. He handed you a book titled, Open Veins of Latin America, by Eduardo Galeano. It chronicles US and European imperialism in the region. I would have slapped him upside his head with the book. However, I expect you to keep my book on your nightstand, right next to the bible and the other book you keep. I believe that title is, "Oh wow, what do I do now?"

You said, "Foreign leaders are more likely to want to cooperate than not cooperate." Do you believe what you say, or are you trying to get

Americans to believe what you say? On August 16, the same raisinette-looking midget said, "Obama is lost in the Andromeda nebula."

Do not listen to people that may get this confused with the Andromeda Galaxy, because it's the same thing. It's merely an older term before Edwin Hubble discovered galaxies. I just made you five-times smarter than you are with no cost to the taxpayers.

Your Obama-Care is dividing this country faster than you can get it swept through congress, simply because it stinks. I don't want the same insurance plan that Ted Kennedy was under. The insurance that civil service has is deplorable, just like the USPO as you rightfully pointed out. Ted Kennedy had seizures and my Mom, who worked for the USPO for over 20-years, is not eligible for hearing aids. If you don't believe me Sir, then pick up your phone and call her on live television. I want the whole world to know how the current plan for civil servants stinks and you are doing nothing except making it worse. You are the President of the United States, so find her telephone number yourself.

The reason it stinks is simply due to the fact it is over 1,000, 2,000 pages and growing. There are more loopholes in this proposed legislation than a tax-cheat's wet dream. This legislation surpassed Pamela Anderson's home movie in the Internet download world.

There is more pork in this bill than what was stuck in Mama Cass's pie-hole.

Where are you going to get the money to support Obama-Care? You promised me, along with millions of other taxpayers that our taxes would not go up; in fact, we would receive a tax decrease. You also promised voters the bill would be crafted in a transparent manner via CSPAN and having republicans assist. Well, do you care to defend your promise to my face? Although fifty people probably watch CSPAN on a daily basis, apparently they spread the word rather quickly there was nothing shown about Obama-care. Once again, you underestimated the will of the people.

As part of the overhaul to the medical FUBAR you have us in, congress is considering putting a tax on sodas and other sugary drinks. Too much sugar packs on weight, thus providing Americans with a greater chance of contracting diabetes. Mr. President, have you seen your pick for Surgeon General? If she's the poster-child for fitness, who was your second pick, Gary Coleman?

Don't stop at putting a tax on only sodas. You should also tax potato chips, KFC, macaroni & cheese, breakfast cereal and all the other crap we eat. Pizza delivered to your house isn't any better for a person than soda! In fact, a person should get an insurance credit if they eat the box.

If you tax all of this stuff, people will become healthier and then you would be one-step closer to achieving your health-care dreams. Moreover, this would generate huge revenue to help pay the 15-million unemployed citizens. It will probably be closer to 16-million when this book is published, but who's counting? Perhaps this is part of his plan.

If you want to preach healthiness, then I suggest you watch CSPAN. By watching CSPAN, you can observe congress people sleeping, drooling, and rolling their eyes, all while butchering the English language. From afar, it looks like any other geriatric ward, but the close-up shots are devastating. You appear to be in shape but here is the list in alphabetical order and my opinion: http://www.house.gov/house/MemberWWW. shtml

Neil Abercrombie-(D-HI)-Grizzly Adams that requires a diet planner
Gary Ackerman-(D-NY)-Not in shape and won't last long
Michelle Bachmann-(R-MN)-Great shape, nice mug!
Tammy Baldwin-(D-WI)-Swelled-up since her Wikipedia picture
Roscoe Bartlett-(R-MD)-I see liver spots
Melissa Bean-(D-IL)-Needs to lay off the beans
Howard Berman-(D-CA)-Maybe one more term
Marion Berry-(D-AR)-Needs a name change and diet pills
Judy Biggert-(R-IL)-Never laugh at your elders
Rob Bishop-(R-UT)-Vegans would kick him out for cheating
Sanford Bishop-(D-GA)-Don't get your fingers next to his teeth
Tim Bishop-(D-NY)-If I look like him at his 60, show me the death panel
Marsha Blackburn-(R-TN)-Michelle Bachman and Marsha-lethal combination
Earl Blumenauer-(D-OR)-Tragically looks like Bill Nye the science guy
John Boehner-(R-Minority Leader)-How do you pronounce the last name?

Jo Bonner-(R-AL)-Wow, two boners. He's eating more than salad

Mary Bono-Mack-(R-CA)-Hotter than Stifler's Mom

John Boozman-(R-AR) His picture and last name seem to fit

Madeleine Bordallo-(D-Guam)-Easy choice for a death panel

Leonard Boswell-(D-IA)-Another term is too risky

Rick Boucher-(D-VA)-Checking to see if the neighbors' kids are missing

Allen Boyd-(D-FL)-Loves the biscuits and gravy at the Waffle House

Bobby Bright-(D-AL)-It's not his bald spot, it's his creepy picture

Michael Burgess-(R-TX)-Not the first doctor I've seen with two chins

G.K. Butterfield-(D-NC)-Has eaten many fields of butter

Dennis Cardoza-(D-CA)-He'll lose the other chin if cuts back on doughnuts

Mike Castle-(R-DE)-Two more terms should do it

Ben Chandler-(D-KY)-Kentucky horses run from Ben

Donna Christensen-(D-Virgin Islands)-Which island is she?

Yvette Clarke-(D-NY)-Blame the pound cake

James Clyburn-(D-SC)-Super-sized his meal more than once

Howard Coble-(Nazi-NC)-Won't finish his term without an oxygen bottle

Gerald Connolly-(D-VA)-More rolls than Dunkin' Doughnuts

Joe Courtney-(D-CT)-If he looks like this at 56, he's doomed

Elijah Cummings-(D-MD)-Leave the crabs alone mister

Danny Davis-(D-IL)-Must love sweet tea

Lincoln Davis-(D-TN)-Should be receiving Medicaid

Nathan Deal-(R-GA)-Looks forward to Thanksgiving, as well as every meal

Rosa Delauro-(D-CT)-Very frightening looking, no mask required

Norman Dicks-(D-WA)-His head is huge, but in proportion with his torso

John Dingell-(D-MI)-My advice to you is to avoid a stress test

Vernon Ehlers-(R-MI) Hope you make it to receive a free copy of my book

Keith Ellison-(D-MN)-Save some bratwurst for the rest

Jo Ann Emerson-(R-MO)-Gorgeous blue eyes and holding together nicely

Eliot Engel-(D-NY)-Somebody hide the kids, real creepy picture

Eni Faleomavaega-(D-America Samoa)–This guy would eat the shell on a coconut

Mary Fallin-(R-OK)-Ride em' cowboy-well preserved, congrats

Sam Farr-(D-CA)-Is that a rug or Grecian formula?

Chaka Fattah-(D-PA)-Fattah than a house

Virginia Foxx–(R-NC)-Cross-eyed or glass eye

Barney Frank–(D-NY)-How many hotdogs did he eat to get those chins

Marcia Fudge–(D-OH)-Named after her favorite desert

Gabrielle Gifford–(D-AZ)-another cutie, but on the wrong side

Alan Grayson-(D-FL)-Lethal combination. Overweight *and* stupid

Al Green-(D-TX)-Looks like Grady from Sanford & Son, but still has dark hair

Raul Grijalva-(D-AZ)-Loves to celebrate Cinco De Mayo–biggin'

Ralph Hall-(R-TX)-Should contact MJ's doctor for oxygen bottles-hang in there

Phil Hare-(D-IL)-Shopping carts cringe, let alone the food isles

Alcee Hastings-(D-FL)-Impeached as a judge, fat and still elected

Mazie Hirono-D-HI)-The hula would shatter her hips

Tim Holden-(D-PA)-Dude, get some sun

Mike Honda-(D-CA)-Must love his rice noodles

Steny Hoyer–(D-MJ Leader) Probably his last term

Sheila Jackson Lee-(D-TX)-Looks as if she would eat a cell phone

Eddie Bernice Johnson-(D-TX)-Would chase a rolling Oreo

Sam Johnson-(R-TX)-Old, but an American hero, God bless

Paul Kanjorski-(D-PA)-Somebody needs to dust him off

Patrick Kennedy-(D-RI)-Nice to see he broke away from OxyContin

Dale Kildee-(D-MI)-I thought Herman Munster was a fictitious character

Carolyn Kilpatrick-(D-MI)-I wonder what Uhura did after Star Trek

Mary Jo Kilroy-(D-OH)-She would kill for a Twinkie

John Larson-(D-CT)-More gaps in his teeth than Mike Tyson

Barbara Lee-(D-CA)-Needs to meet Sarah Lee

Sander Levin-(D-MI)-Never said no to Colonel Sanders

Charles Lewis-(R-CA)-He should be praying I'm not judging ethics

John Lewis-(D-GA)-I bet he has attended more than one barbeque

John Linder-(R-GA)-Look at the jowls on his mug

Nita Lowey-(D-NY)-After looking at her, inita drink

Frank Lucas-(R-OK)-Judging by his headshot, he's above a middleweight

Cynthia Lummis-(R-WY)-A reason to visit Wyoming, well preserved

Donald Manzullo-(R-IL)-Spare tire syndrome

Kenny Marchant-(R-TX)-Ate the 64-ouncer in record time

Jerrold Nadler-(D-NY)-Could easily eat the big apple

Grace Napolitano-(D-CA)-Elected at the age of 62-should have retired

Randy Neugebauer-(R-TX)-Thankfully, cows can outrun him

Jim Oberstar-(D-MN)-His great grandchildren miss him

John Olver-(D-MA)-His last term too, good Lord

Solomon Ortiz-(D-TX)-Three in a row that are 72-years old-we need term limits

Bill Pascrell-(D-NJ)-Oops, make that four in a row.....good God!

Ed Pastor-(D-AZ)-Looks like he could manhandle a buffet

Ron Paul-(R/L-TX)-Let it go Ron, just let it go

Donald Payne-(D-NJ)-Forks run and hide when he enters the kitchen

Nancy Pelosi-(Speaker of the House)-Speaking is not her strong point

Gary Peters-(D-MI)-More chins than Chinatown

Collin Peterson-(D-MN)-Looks like a buffet man

Chellie Pingree-(D-ME)-Not even the moose are safe

David Price-(D-NC)-Run Forest, run

Charles Rangel-(D-NY)-Boo! Did you think I was the taxman? Enjoys free meals

Laura Richardson-(D-CA)-She could scare a scarecrow

Silvestre Reyes-(D-TX)-Ain't no mountain high enough.....to cover his shadow

Hal Rogers-(R-KY)-Priorities are right, but the sole reason why sporks were invented

Ileana Ros-Lehtinen-(R-FL)-Is that a dangling chad or chin?

Dutch Ruppersberger-(D-MD)-Likes Dutch ovens and burgers

Bobby Rush-(D-IL)-Been to every restaurant on Rush Street.....in two nights

Gregorio Sablan-(I-Mariana Islands)-More than one island in case he slips

Linda Sanchez-(D-CA)-On a deserted island with her, you're the meal

Loretta Sanchez-(D-CA)-Healthier looking than Linda….in a good way

Jim Sensenbrenner-(R-WI)-Put down the cheese and get back to work

Carol Shea-Porter-(D-NH)-Looks like a former president of the NOW organization

John Shimkus-(R-IL)-If he's only fifty-one, then I'm thirteen

Albio Sires-(D-NJ)-He said, "pass the gravy" more than once last week

Ike Skelton-(D-MO)-He should be a skeleton in about four years, God bless

Louise Slaughter-(D-NY)-Last name suggests the decrease in pigeons in New York

John Spratt-(D-SC)-Definitely a heavy weight contender

Pete Stark-(D-CA)-Will he live long enough to see Obama-Care?

John Tanner-(D-TN)-The reason why deer can run so fast

Harry Teague-(D-NM)-Moobs and chins

Benny Thompson-(D-MS)-Repeat after me, "*Exercise.*"

Glenn Thompson-(R-PA)-Soup is not in his vocabulary

Dina Titus-(D-NE)-Hasn't seen a *Titus* in about thirty years…

Tim Walz-(D-MN)-Eat more sour kraut and put down the sausages

Maxine Waters-(D-CA)-Try drinking some water….isn't it retirement age

Diane Watson-(D-CA)-Apparently, she ran unopposed

Henry Waxman-(D-CA)-Another reason for term limits, despite decent shape at 69

Lynn Woosley-(D-CA)-If you like gray hair, then checkout this beauty!

Don Young-(R-AK)-Surviving a fight with a polar bear is 50-50-this guy is big

As you can see, the list I compiled only included House Members. I only listed individuals who I think are out of shape, too old, or cuties. It does not include individuals that look evil, or have a *pedophile smile*. I tried to be subjective in my opinions, but as you can see, all the hotties are republicans. I think I know why the democrats want your health-care system implemented. Can you imagine how their families look?

The average age of our congressional representatives is 55-years, which is higher than the previous century; therefore, do you really think they have a grip on our current societal issues? People that are 55-years old are in touch, but it's the people in their 70's that scare me. Most people in their 70's have a hard time driving and get dizzy for no apparent reason. How can they hear the voice of the people when they have a hard time hearing?

Would you do me a favor Mr. President? Before you jack-up my taxes, would you mind sending me a signed poster of <u>Michelle Bachmann</u>, <u>Mary Bono-Mack</u>, *Marsha Blackburn,* <u>Jo Ann Emerson</u>, <u>Mary Fallin</u> and <u>Cynthia Lummis</u>?

They can wear their normal attire, because I don't want you to think I'm requesting anything freaky. If you tell them it's for me, it won't be an issue. Do not mention the names of Edwards, Vitter, Spitzer, Ensign, or Sanford. Otherwise, they may get nervous.

PS –Ladies, keep up the great work in each of your states and email me at the usual address. Keep it clean in case my wife reads the email.

It would be wrong of me to include House Members and not our beloved Senators. If you think House Members are the main reason for refills on oxygen bottles and recertification of AED's around the Capitol, you would be surprised. In case you're not familiar with medical terms, AED is an acronym for automated external defibrillator.

I hold Senators to a higher standard, so their looks, or lack thereof, is not of great importance, but sleeping while on CSPAN is a national embarrassment. This should be exciting, are you ready Mr. President?

<u>Daniel Akaka</u>-(D-HI)-Needs a name change and is 84-years old. How far do you think he would get if he had to swim to work?

Lamar Alexander-(R-TN)-Filled Fred Thompson's position in 2003. Lamar plays the piano, only 69-years old and worked with President Nixon in his early years-good job

<u>John Barrasso</u>-(R-WY)-Squeaky clean and only 57. Assumed his office in 2007-it gets better Senator, hang in there and keep pounding away!

Max Baucus-(D-MT)-The best word to describe this man is tainted. If I believed everything written in Wikipedia, I would think this man is the antichrist. That's why I use Bing.com.

Evan Bayh-(D-IN)-Assumed the position (LOL) in 1999. Besides his political affiliation, I can't find any dirt. The good news is, he's only 53.

Mark Begich-(D-AK)-Only 47-years old-I wonder if he tricks the older Senators to take him to Walt Disney World after getting them to believe he is their lost grandchild.

Michael Bennett-(D-CO)-Only 44-years old, but something is strange. Despite being a Democrat, he appears to be extremely smart-must be cheating from the Republicans during tests.

Obama- Can you introduce me to Senator Begich? I would actually like to meet this man, because of his previous professions. He's either really smart or they couldn't find anybody else in Colorado. Oh never mind Obama-call me Michael-I'm at the same number. We can talk studio stuff.....

Robert Bennett-(R-UT)-A spry 75-years old, Robert appears to be all over the map like a blue line in his political views. He is one of three Republicans who voted against the Flag Desecration Amendment. I think it's time for him to retire, or change party affiliation.

Jeff Bingaman-(D-NM)-65-years old and believes in *going green*. He believes in a cap & trade policy and reducing greenhouse gases. Time for you to retire Sir, your work is done.

Christopher Bond-(R-MO)-Will not be seeking office in 2010. His son returned home safely after two tours in Iraq. Congrats Senator-your son is a hero. Please thank him for me. Tell your critics (REP) they would not be paying higher prices in gasoline if we drilled offshore, as you proposed. God's speed Sir.

Barbara Boxer-(D-CA)-Primary reason for me leaving California-She makes Nancy Pelosi look conservative and cute. OK, back from heaving....next!

Sherrod Brown-(D-OH)-I hate Akron! Sherrod looks like he went to the bathroom in his pants and trying to hide it from the photographer.

Sam Brownback-(R-KS)-Not seeking reelection in 2010, which is fine with me. However, it may be bad for Kansas, because he may run for Governor.

Jim Bunning-(R-KY)-He is 77-years old and planning on running again in 2010. I'm sure you can retire Sir, correct? Good grief, give somebody else a chance.

Richard Burr-(R-NC)-He may be the 12th cousin of Aaron Burr. Perhaps, I am the 16th second cousin, once removed. He supports the death penalty, good job Senator

Roland Burris-(D-IL)-Hmm, he appears to be an ethical and standup citizen; I don't know of any hoodlums or scumbags that came from IL-Oops, not according to Bing.com

Robert Byrd-(D-WV)-Helped build the pyramids and was the fist to use fire-Good Lord; it is time you take a breather…from the oxygen tank and take Mark B. to WDW.

Maria Cantwell-(D-WA)-Ask her advice on how to secure money for campaign finance, because she seems somewhat knowledgeable… Don't put her on an ethics committee

Benjamin Cardin-(D-MD)-Only 65-years old, yet he has been in politics since I was 7-years old. Senator, can you find something else to do, like retire?

Thomas Carper-(D-DE)-How could you avoid golfing with Paula Parkinson? It was a great political move, but she could have kissed your balls for good luck, but I guess you'll never know- her mug needed some work, yet Dan Quayle probably couldn't tell us what color her eyes were, let alone spell the color

Robert Casey-(D-PA)-Record time in receiving a heart and liver transplant-Oops, he died, wrong Robert-(He was the governor of PA) His son, Robert Casey Jr. is the Senator from PA.

Saxby Chambliss-(R-GA)-I think he's one of the most despicable Senators ever-Saxby, when you have time, please visit me at the National Vietnam War Museum in Orlando, FL-I have some friends that would love to meet you

Tom Coburn-(R-OK)-A true Republican-thanks Senator and keep up the good work

Thad Cochran-(R-MS)-Was on the cheerleading squad with Trent Lott at the University of Mississippi and I think that's a little creepy-I bet you can't do the splits at the age of 71 without shattering some bones

Susan Collins-R-ME)-Keep up the good work Senator-I've never been to Maine, so if you can arrange to yank Nancy Pelosi's plane away from her, will you fly me to your state? I noticed you're not married, so my wife said I can't fly alone, therefore I need two seats. Email me at fly-my-florida-hunk-to-maine.net

Kent Conrad-(D-ND)-Can you have Angelo Mozilo give me a call? I am upside down in my payments. Oh, he's no longer in charge-Do you have any suggestions Senator?

Bob Corker-(R-TN)-Do you have additional wetlands for sale? Wal-Mart is looking to build another big box in Orlando-Also, if I find those missing papers while you were Mayor, I'll let you know-can you do me a favor and send photos of your daughters?

John Cornyn-(R-TX)-Do you have any neighbors that married a box turtle? You should have known the Daily Show would jump on that comment. I got your point, but it was a bad analogy. I would have said, "It does not affect your daily life very much if your neighbor marries a corpse." (That's because you can't hear the screaming)

Mike Crapo-(R-IN)-Smart thinking by putting a macro over the *a* in your name while running for office. Continued success and a quick recovery.....God's speed Senator.

Jim Demint-(R-SC)-Married his high school sweetheart. Continued success and great work Senator-I believe in the same set of personal values regarding who's teaching our children, but at least you had the guts to say it. Keep pushing on-

Christopher Dodd-(D-CT)-Good grief, can you retire? FMLA is killing companies and can you count how many controversies that claims your involvement? I lost count-I think you are a bad seed. What was the kid's name in The Omen, oh yeah, Damien.

Byron Dorgan-(D-ND)-A democrat with Republican values. Dude, go ahead and change parties; it's the fad these days.

Richard Durbin-(D-IL)-The Sierra Club gave him a 90% rating on environmental issues, which leads me to believe that he needs to retire.

John Ensign(R-NV)-An alleged born again Christian who recently acknowledged he was pounding somebody other than his wife. Time

for you to go Sir-However, I'm having a hard time finding the right Cynthia Hampton on the Internet. Is your wife the fat brown-haired woman or your mistress?

Michael Enzi-(R-WY)-Good work Senator, but don't you feel like sleeping-in more often as you age? Let somebody else take a stab at it.

Russell Feingold-(D-WY)-Found creative and affective ways of beating his opponents in his 1992, 1998 and 2004 races. He believes in Universal Health Care. We are all entitled to our opinions, but mine are always right. Senator-Don't touch my Insurance!

Dianne Feinstein-(D-CA)-The second reason why I left California. Can you retire woman? Good grief, just look at yourself

Al Franken-(D-MN)-Great, now we have a half-baked comedian in office. Hey Al, do you have any advice on back taxes? Better yet, do you have any good jokes?

Kirsten Gillibrand-(D-NY)-The youngest Senator at the age of 42 and appears not to mind wearing makeup. However, makeup doesn't cover her liberal views. Do not let the pound cake sneak up on you Kirsten.

Lindsey Graham-(R-SC)-Other than having a 0% approval rating from the gay community, I don't see any issues. Keep up the good work Senator.

Chuck Grassley-(R-IA)-Please do not run again in 2010-Time to give the job to somebody in his or her 60's. Thanks for the good work and enjoy your retirement.

Judd Gregg-(R-NH)-The University of New Hampshire renamed one of its buildings to Gregg Hall. I think that's due to them securing $266 million in federal funds for meteorological and atmospheric studies. Good grief, quit wasting my money and listen to your weatherman!

Kay Hagan-(D-NC)-She can't do any harm, because she represents North Dakota. What do those people do? I know you believe in God Kay. The ad that Dole ran was wrong.

Tom Harkin-(D-IA)-Your work is done. Good Lord, do you even remember what an airplane looks like, let alone fly one? Did you fly the F-4 in Japan, Cuba, or Vietnam? Could you have mistaken that gaffe for the Hindenburg?

Orrin Hatch-(R-UT)-I've always admired Orrin Hatch; however Sir, it's time to retire. Your work is done and I assume you have paid for a copy of Java for your website. Take care Orrin and if you care to invite me to Utah, make sure it is not Salt Lake City. That town is creepy!

Kay Bailey Hutchison-(R-TX)-She is one reason why you don't mess with Texas. Good luck on your Governor run, I'm sure you'll get it. Let's have a barbeque and head over to the gun range for desert.

James Inhofe-(R-OK)-You're right Senator, global warming is a hoax. Your time is done and you served the people well. Please let somebody under fifty take a stab at it.

Daniel Inouye-(D-HI)-Just look at you Senator! Your time was up a decade ago. Did you work on the Roman Coliseum? Regardless, you're an American hero. You are a decorated hero from WWII. I did not see any awards from the Civil War.

Johnny Isakson-(R-GA)-Nice work Senator-keep it up-it's refreshing to see somebody on the *right side* of the issues

Mike Johanns-(R-NE)-Fresh meat in the Senate. My advice to you Senator is to do the complete opposite the seasoned Senators do. It's not the amount of committees you are on, but the ones you choose. You fight the fight you are fighting. Would you rather box a kid in a wheelchair, or Mike Tyson and his friends? That is my advice and good luck.

Tim Johnson-(D-SD)-.Tell your son thanks for his patriotism and congratulations on a healthy return to work ~ sincerely-

Edward Kaufman-(D-DE)-Filling Biden's seat, which should not be hard-gone in 2010

Edward Kennedy-(D-MA)-An absolute picture of health! Ted, I'm over here Sir. Rumors have it that Ted's next book will be aptly titled, *Submersion* –time for a nap Sir?

John Kerry-(D-MA)-Senator, I think you're nothing more than a Jane Fonda in a suit. You said, "If you don't, you get stuck in Iraq." It appears that if you're not making a blunder when addressing reporters, you're involved in some type of controversy.

Amy Klobuchar-(D-MN)-Senator-What was your most embarrassing moment in politics? Was it getting Al Franken on your team or pledging your vote to Obama as a super-delegate?

Herb Kohl-(D-WI)-People this rich (estimated at $300MM) are normally not in touch with society, let alone anything else.

Jon Kyl-(R-AZ)-Jon is 67-years old and is the junior Senator in Arizona-good grief! However, he's done an impeccable job and is good for one more term-continued success!

Mary Landrieu-(D-LA)-She co-authored the Hurricane Katrina Disaster Relief and Economic Recovery Act of 2005. There was more pork in that request than a butcher shop. I believe she was the catalyst for Paula Abdul's *Cold Hearted Snake*. I wonder if I can buy her vote for $100-million.....

Frank Lautenberg-(D-NJ)-Frank is 85 years old and our second oldest Senator. Good day Sir, your job is done. Do I need to scream this to you, or is your vision okay?

Patrick Leahy-(D-VT)-Patrick is 69 years old and has served as the Senator of Vermont since 1975. At his age, he should be collecting maple syrup or taking naps.

Carl Levin-(D-MI)-Good Lord, can you retire too Sir? Thanks for your ongoing service to the country, but trust me, those daily naps are right around the corner.

Joseph Lieberman-(ID-CT)-He's always reminded me of the short guy from the Penn and Teller act. Stay away from John Hagee please. Would you like Medicaid, Medical or the Obama plan Sir?

Blanche Lincoln-(D-AR)-The only thing we have in common is our age.

Richard Lugar-(R-IN)-Richard is 77-years old and God bless him; he still has his teeth. He is a true Republican from my father's home state. Senator, before any sort of dementia sets-in, take an early retirement and call it a day. Enjoy life for a change.

Mel Martinez-(R-FL)-He's gone.

John McCain-(R-AZ)-The senior Senator of Arizona is 72-years old. He is a true American Hero. I voted for you Sir, but people wanted change and change they got. With the deepest respect-Keep pushing on Sir, because I know you still have the fight within you. Thanks for all of your philanthropic work that you and your wife have done.

Claire McCaskill-(D-MO)-She likes to twitter. Apparently, she is the second-most followed member of congress on Twitter. Is this how we grade our elected officials? If they twitter, does their popularity rise? My pet monkey knows how to twitter.

Mitch McConnell-(R-KY)-If I lived in Kentucky, I would be a drunk. I've been there often and they have the finest bourbon in the world. I wonder if the Senator partakes in a little hooch now and again. Please send some Senator......I'm running low....send to the usual address ~ thanks!

Robert Menendez-(D-NJ)-If I could ask you one question Senator, it would be, what have you accomplished since being on the subcommittee for Public Lands and Forests?

Jeff Merkley-(D-OR)-He co-authored The Healthy Americans Act (HAA). We should have an American Fitness Poster and I recommend Ted Kennedy and Robert Byrd to become our fitness idols.

Barbara Mikulski-(D-MD)-I can't make fun of old ladies.

Lisa Murkowski(R-AK)-The internet trolls can be cruel with your pictures, can't they cupcake? I like the picture of you in 2004 with the Capitol in the background.

Patty Murray-(D-WA)-Speaking of cruel, Patty reminds me of Andy Warhol

Ben Nelson-(D-NE)-Only 68-years old and graying evenly.

Bill Nelson-(D-FL)-All it takes is one trip to space to change the way one thinks. Let's send him back for another ride.

Mark Pryor-(D-AR)-He is living proof that you don't have to pass an IQ test to be in the Senate. (That was his line, not mine)

Jack Reed-(D-RI)-If it wasn't for his service in the Military, I would have nothing to say. Despite our opposing views, you seem like a nice guy-there, I feel better

Harry Reid-(D-NV)-Only 69-years old, but he looks rough. Senator, don't they have Bingo in Las Vegas-Relax and retire. I think Harry suffers from dementia, because nobody is this spastic and maintains a job.

James Risch-(R-ID)-Somebody had to fill Larry Craig's seat, get it?

Pat Roberts-(R-KS)-Only 73-years old and has conservative values. Good job, now retire please.

John Rockefeller IV-(D-WV)-72-years old and signs of Alzheimer's. As opposed to relaxing at his ranch in Wyoming, he resides in Charleston, WV-go figure

Bernard Sanders-(I-VT)-In 2003, the Senator told Alan Greenspan that he was out of touch-how's the economy now Mr. In-Touch? Are you still blaming Bush?

Charles Schumer-(D-NY)-His competition in 1998 was Geraldine Ferraro. A 3-legged horse would have beaten both. He opposed Clinton's impeachment-enough said

Jeff Sessions-(R-AL)-More controversies swirl around this man than brownie crumbs on a fat woman-retire Sir and move onto something else

Jeanne Shaheen-(D-NH)-She is the average age of a senator, 62-years old.

Richard Shelby-(R-AL)-75-years young-He was one of ten republican senators that voted for an acquittal on Bill Clinton's perjury charges. Senator, were you watching the same interview as the rest of the nation? *"I did not have sexual relations with that woman."* Yeah, I'd deny having any sexual relations with that hog.

Olympia Snowe-(R-ME)-Great job Senator-keep it up-and save me from the death panel

Arlen Spector-(D-PA)-79-years old and can't remember if he's a Republican or a Democrat. He does not know how to hold town meetings, good grief Senator; retire

Debbie Stabenow-(D-MI)-You're at a disadvantage because of your home state. I would move and start over, but if you stay there, then good luck!

John Tester-(D-MT)-We're almost the same age, but he asserted, "There's no more middle class" in reference to the Bush administration. Senator, there were more millionaires under Clintons' watch. It's nice to know history. You should read about it.

John Thune-(R-SD)-Too young to have any dirt on him-Senator, did you ever inhale?

Mark Udall-(D-CO)-Has climbed more mountains than what he has accomplished thus far as a Senator.

David Vitter-(R-LA)-God forgave you Senator? My wife would never take that for an excuse. Which God do you use?

George Voinovich-(R-OH)-73-years young-I'm sorry to hear you grew up in Cleveland. My condolences Senator—seriously—I lived in Akron, but I escaped.

Mark Warner-(D-VA)-He promised not to raise taxes while campaigning in 2001, but tried to raise them in 2002. Gee, that sounds familiar.

Jim Webb-(D-VA)-Despite his heroism in Vietnam; I feel he was out of line with President Bush. Regardless, they kissed and made up. I also contend the picture of them is hanging on somebody's wall and not the former President's.

Sheldon Whitehouse-(D-RI)-In 2007, he ranked as the number two most liberal Senator. That is nothing to be proud of Sir-you should always strive for number one.

Roger Wicker-(R-MS)-Governor Haley Barbour appointed Wicker to feel Trent Lott's place. He hasn't had much time to do anything.

Ron Wyden-(D-OR)-He characterizes himself as an "independent voice for Oregonians and the nation." That translates to sitting on the fence on every issue. Don't speak for me Senator-thanks.

There you have it Mr. President. That's your team. Did you ever watch the movie, *Dodge ball*? I love that line, "If you can dodge a wrench, then you can dodge a ball." How many of your team members can dodge a wrench if one was heaved at them? If you're looking for somebody to be the thrower, I'm your man. I could hit ten people with one throw, especially if the wrench careened off an oxygen bottle. However, you didn't pick these people. They either already had the position, or they were elected on the same day as you.

Here is the team you picked:

Joseph Biden-(VP)-The ultimate gaffe-machine. The shot heard around the world was when he was campaigning in Missouri and said, "Chuck, stand up, let the people see you. Oh, God love ya. What am I talking about?" Missourians knew their State Senator Chuck Graham is a paraplegic, but people viewing youtube know him as *the cripple*.

Hillary Clinton-(Secretary of Sate)-She gives cause for every woman to burn their pantsuits. I don't want to see her in a mini-skirt, but her dreadful attire is gut wrenching to put it mildly. Her voice is like fingernails on a chalkboard, but when she hits the high notes, blood gushes from my ears.

PS We almost had an international incident when Hillary recently went to Africa. She has a right to speak her mind, but she represents the United States. I thought her head was going to start spinning around while spitting out guacamole.

Timothy Geithner-(Secretary of the Treasury)-How hard is this job? What are we down to, as a nation; a few gold bars in Fort Knox? He can count our money on an abacus that is missing beads. He was the only one confirmed by the senate, because the first two nominees backed out. Annette Nazareth would have done a good job. In case you were not aware Sir, she was the former Commissioner of the US SEC from 2005-2008. That's when companies such as Lehman Brothers, among several others took a dive.

Robert Gates-(Secretary of Defense)-Smart move to keep this man. Mr. Gates accepted his position in 2006, but he was the former Director of the CIA, so it would behoove you to not mess with him. People with his knowledge scare me. **Boo!**

Eric Holder-(Attorney General)-Mr. President, do you concur with your esteemed colleague that we are a nation of cowards when discussing race relations? That's what Mr. Holder said while speaking at an event during black history month. Maybe he was speaking for himself, but definitely not for me. If I ever get in trouble, would you have this gent give me a pardon? Oh never mind, you're the President, so you have the same powers, correct? I think Mr. Holder and you should read the constitution. Read Article II, Section II. Somebody has abused their powers.

Kenneth Salazar-(Secretary of the Interior)-Oh God, another member from the infamous *gang of fourteen*. Regardless, this position oversees our National Parks, Land Management, The Bureau of Indian Affairs, along with a couple more useless departments. What is so hard about Indian Affairs? I don't think they have any reservations about their reservations. However, if you can do me a favor, please direct Mr.

Salazar to turn the water on in Huron, CA. All he has to do is turn a knob. If you give me the permission, I will fly there and do it myself. Do you watch the news? I believe this falls under Land Management, if not, how would you best describe those words?

Mr. President-Would you like to meet the extremely funny comedian, Paul Rodriguez? I can make this happen. All you have to do is help me turn on the water in this farming community and you and I will both be stars. This may get you reelected. Well, I doubt it, but you have nothing to lose at this point.

Thomas Vilsack-(Secretary of Agriculture)-OK, how important is this job? This position is either going to be attacked by farmers or The Organic Consumers Association. I know plenty of farmers and they are hardworking, tough and a staple of America's great frontier. I guess an analogy would be who would you least want to face in an alley. Would you rather face a fatheaded drooling kid or a polar bear?

Mr. Vilsack-Please give my utmost respect to every farmer you know---sincerely...and thanks!

Gary Locke-(Secretary of Commerce)-Oh dear Lord, please forgive me for any Chinese jokes that may have offended the good secretary. I completely forgot, but the jokes need to stay. I can't erase a few jokes because you picked one Chinaman on your cabinet. Now I know what it's like to be J. Biden.

Mr. Locke was the optimum pick, because we get most of our garbage from China.

Don't you agree with me? I bet the collection of CD's you gave the British Prime Minister came from China, along with fingerprints from the children who put them into their individual wrappings.

What happened to Bill Richardson? I would have picked him too, because he seems like a standup man. Oops, hold on while I finish reading what pay to play means. Interestingly enough, I never would have guessed that politicians would even entertain such a thing.

Hilda Solis-(Secretary of Labor)-Wow, that was a close one Mr. President. Timing is everything. Thank goodness the check did not bounce.

Mrs. Solis, would you like to meet Paul Rodriguez? He's Hispanic too and I think you two have more in common than you think. Since you're the Secretary of Labor, can you give me a job? I want to be the person in charge of water in Huron, CA. Can you make that happen? I love Mexican food and I will be forever grateful. Gracias, y tu eres muy bonita! Did I get that right?

Kathleen Sebelius-(Secretary of Health and Human Services)-Gee, another person with an "unintentional error" in their taxes. I think she slashed the State's educational system by $7MM. How can anyone be this cruel to our children?

It then dawned on me that the only famous people to come out Kansas were Bob Dole and Fatty Arbuckle. What are the chances of Kansas producing another Einstein? It turned out to be a good choice to take money from the educational department.

Shaun Donovan-(Secretary of HUD)-There is enough foreclosures on the market to put every homeless person in a home. I believe this department helps the homeless and I can't think of a better win-win situation. I would love to have another schizophrenic living on the other side of me. This would allow my two neighbors to slap the crap out of each other all day, instead of my one neighbor who only swats at invisible things.

Raymond LaHood-(Secretary of Transportation)-You are not going to scare anybody by picking a person who looks like Martin Scorsese to run this department. Tell Mr. LaHood that I am keeping my SUV, plane, helicopter, freighter, yacht, nuclear aircraft carrier and skateboard.

Steven Chu-(Secretary of Energy)-Damn, two Chinamen? I'm sorry Mr. President, I didn't know. This man has split the atom, thus he's qualified. The best news is that he owes no taxes and looks smart. Can you imagine squaring off with Mr. Chu on Jeopardy? For the sake of the country, don't do it Mr. President. However, the mere thought of you playing Jeopardy and losing on a hundred dollar question regarding US Politics would be a Kodak moment.

Arne Duncan-(Secretary of Education)-Where's his credentials! He played basketball for a living! Oh, I see that he is from Chicago and worked for Richard M. Daley as the CEO of Chicago public schools. Richard M. Daley has more baggage than O'Hare airport. Now I know why I cannot afford the parking meters in that town.

Eric Shinseki-(Secretary of Veterans Affairs)-This man has credentials! He has a Purple Heart, Ranger Tab, Parachutist Badge, oh please….A Parachutist badge? Does he also have a knot-tying badge? Thanks for your service General.

Janet Napolitano-(Secretary of Homeland Security)-Good God almighty! She looks like Judge Napolitano from Foxx news. (Sorry Judge) For the Darwinians, I found your missing link. There is a little right-wing extremism memo controversy flap that started around April, but what's a little flap? Do you still think she was a good pick? If I were she, I would be nervous if there was a death panel.

This does not include your list of insipid czars. You have as many czars as you do teeth! The word czar has a negative connotation and you're building your cast of useless czars faster than a Chinaman eats from a bowl. In your situation, I would at least have a czar for getting your butt out of hot water. Oh wait, you have Robert Gibbs and I've never seen a better white tap-dancer.

The term czar is silly. Why couldn't you find it within yourself to be different and get rid of the name in its entirety? However, since you're a sheep and not a leader, I understand. I also understand that not all of your czars report to you directly, so you should hire me to be your czar of czars! I would slap the others into shape and make sure they're doing something! It is impossible for you to know what they do each day. It is obvious you can't keep track of the Speaker of the House. I'm not going to list each one, because the only person who would gain any knowledge from the list of czars and what they do is you Sir.

That's not only your team Mr. President, but it is America's team. Do you think you made the best choices possible? I agree with a few, but not the rest. Yet, I am not the one who sought office. The job is not easy is it? Today is August 26, 2009 and although you have been in office for a short time, you picked the perfect time to go on vacation. What is another two trillion in debt the taxpayers must repay?

You will not get the money you need from your proposed cap & trade policy, because the American people will oppose that as well. Besides, by the time you are finished putting our country into the abyss, we should be down to roughly one-million homeowners. The rest of us will be living in our cars, tents, or with the in-laws. When people find out they may have to live with their in-laws, it will make our first revolutionary war look like band-camp.

The people wanted change, which is what you promised. I did not vote for you, but the majority of the citizens did. I had a flashback when Jimmy Carter was our President; therefore, it made my decision easy. Polls indicate you are not doing a good job, but a blind squirrel can point that out. The Rasmussen poll for today shows the American public (drum-roll please) has a 50% disapproval rating. When you took office, 30% disapproved. If that is not taking a beating, go ask the Los Angles Clippers. They're familiar with beatings. Wait until your socialized medical plan doesn't pass, then you're going to tank like a rock.

You are my President, but just because I do not like your policies, it does not mean you have expunged the loyalty to my country. Neither you, nor any other democrat can obliterate my deep-seated patriotism. I will always love my country. I will also continue to support our omnipresent troops. None of us like war Mr. President, but our men and women in the military need 100% of your support and I fail to see that from you as well.

Reportedly, you have met with top executives from for-profit health insurance industry thirty-five times in February. How many times have you met with our veterans or our troops? You're busy trying to ramrod a medical plan that does not work down the throats of Americans and you are leaving our troops and veterans behind. They protect you, our rights and most importantly, America.

Were you any good as a community organizer? From what I have observed thus far regarding your presidency, you could not organize a pair of eyeglasses for a blind person.

You may not like my condescending tone and may think my humor is adolescent at best, but that is what makes this country beautiful. There is no other place like America on Earth. In one day's time, I can assert my own opinion, visit a stripper, go to the ocean and eat like Rosie O'Donnell. (I have no idea what she eats, but I thought it was a funny line)

Ted Kennedy's death came at an unfortunate time, because I already wrote about him. I do not want to erase what I wrote about him. Unfortunately, by the time this book is published, a few more politicians may hit the dirt. I am not trying to sound crass, rude or mean in anyway, but I do not have an eraser. The economy has caused me to cutback on many nonessentials.

You stated Mr. President that Ted Kennedy was the greatest senator of your time. With that said, who do you think was the worst during your time? We had some lousy ones, so would you mind commenting?

Politicians are similar to family. They are a close-knit group, despite their differences. As in any family, there are smart and well-revered family members. It does not matter if he or she is a cousin, brother, aunt, etc. Conversely, there is always the redheaded stepchild analogy. It appears that in most families, there is at least one drunken, womanizing dolt.

Most importantly Mr. President, I'm glad that Joseph Biden didn't say, "Ted, stand up, let the people see you. Oh, God love ya. What am I talking about?" when he said a eulogy for Mr. Kennedy.

Regardless, I take offense to what his grandchildren, nieces and nephews said at Mr. Kennedy's funeral service. Despite the fact that Mr. Kennedy was the *Lion of the Senate* for liberals and he accomplished great things for democrats, I feel these children were *pimped-out*. David Shuster from MSNBC had to apologize for saying *pimped-out* when he was talking about Chelsea Clinton, but I do not have to apologize to anyone for my opinion.

How many funerals have you attended when a grandchild or nephew rattled-off *Universal Health Care?* I assert that the timing of these utterances were not coincidental. Our country is in a gridlock over healthcare and the notion that a child would choose their grandfather's words about healthcare is bizarre at best. Although the youngsters lost a grandfather, do they even know the difference between the Republican and Democratic philosophies?

Who asked the children to read from their prepared papers? Was it you, Nancy Pelosi, the Kennedy family or the DNC? Someone or a group (Perhaps, Whitehouse Officials) told those children what to say, which is indisputable. This will not help your cause, but only hurt it. Whoever wrote those comments and asked the children to read them should be ashamed. This democratic tactic has failed in the past.

Ted Kennedy did great things, but he also did bad things. This is not the time to delve into them, because I am running low on paper. Please allow me a few minutes to reflect upon the great things he did for this nation. I feel a lot better now and may Ted's soul rest in peace. From a political perspective only, if Mr. Kennedy was the Lion, then Mr. McCain is the roar.

Regardless of my political affiliation, my heart goes out to his loved ones and his family. I know what it is like to lose somebody close and I wish no ill will or contempt to any of his family members. Naturally, they would know him better than any critic, pundit or naysayer. He is no longer suffering and in a much better place.

America is afloat in turbulent waters, with no lifeguard in site. The Statue of Liberty is ashamed, because she no longer reflects her symbolism. The loss of her symbolism was not your doing. She became embarrassed decades ago. The unraveling of her majestic and tranquil powers was eroded by decades of American liberalism.

As a country, we would rather hand out free needles to pathetic jackals and put too much credence into the Hollywood ideology, as opposed to helping one another. We have become a country for blaming others, as opposed to providing solutions to problems. We would rather give money to the National Endowment for the Arts, as opposed to malnourished kids. Every time our country donates to the NEA, it becomes a *FUBAR*.

This year, the US is donating $185-million dollars to a worthless organization. Why is it worthless Mr. President? It's because nobody has the guts to tell an artist their work is nothing but rubbish. Well, I'll be the person. Art is subjective and I understand it, just as any two-year old in America. However, artists who want to make a mockery out of taxpayer's money are an abomination to our system.

Why do we worship Hollywood and its stable of creatures? Big Brother, Doctor Phil, and Jerry Springer have become babysitters to spoiled children, stay-at-home moms and people with fascination for ridiculous shows. Now I have a chance to make Oprah's Book Club, albeit a small one.

The Hollywood elite helped shove you into office, but where are they now? Has Ron Howard made a 4-minute sequel to his first video? I'm sure you recall the video. How can anybody forget that farce? I haven't heard much from the people that touted they voted for you, or even endorsed you, but the polls suggest why they are quiet. It's as though you have a contagious decease.

Today is Thanksgiving Day, 2009 and the Rasmussen poll shows you having a 34% overall approval rating. I'm a believer, but I can't believe what you have done to this country in such a short period of time. By all accounts, Americans will vote you and your party (The Special Olympians) out of office in 2012.

Mr. President, if you want your popularity to rise, you must create jobs and prosperity for the people. Health care is not the answer. By creating jobs, you will not only raise revenue for the country, but also put self-worth back into the vocabularies of the unemployed. You should be ashamed for making health care your priority. Would you rather have a cavity or a job?

How could you possibly accept the Nobel Peace Price? You were on the job for two weeks when nominated. I would really like to hear from your lips what makes you think you are deserving of such a prestigious award. You should have declined for the reason I just stated.

You didn't do anything during your first two weeks in office other than give Samantha Power a job and bickered like a child with Rush Limbaugh. Samantha has quite the mouth on her, doesn't she? I don't like what she writes, let alone what she says. Never pick an argument with Rush, because you will lose. If you're that confident, then go onto his show. If you don't want to do his show, then do mine. Please?

Your first State of the Union Address was a tragedy. You talked as though you were running for office and mimicked the speech you gave in February of 2009. You failed the fix the economy and told the world that China was beating us at fixing their economy. Sir, if you followed their lead a year ago, we wouldn't have 10-15 million people unemployed!

Why you were pedaling Obama Care like crack, the Chinese reportedly pumped $586-billion into their economy all at the same time. Moreover, the money was for infrastructure jobs only. This put millions of people back to work. This is what caused their economy to leap by a 9% growth by the 3rd quarter of 2009. You're spending money like a drunk at a strip-joint.

You cannot throw one dollar here and one dollar there and expect to put people back to work. Where did the money go? Well, some went to resurfacing tennis courts in Alameda, CA. That's where some of it went. The money is tracked and all you have to do is punish the people that don't spend it properly. I'm sure you know a guy named Tony-Two-Toes, since you're from Chicago. If you don't understand what the American people are trying to tell you, maybe you understand what I'm trying to say. American heard your voice, now listen to mine. Senator Scott Brown from Massachusetts is living proof that America had enough with you and your socialistic viewpoints.

However, I would be remiss if I did not say thank you. If I ever hear another political figure use the word change, I will vote for the other person.

Thank you for listening to my concerns and may God Bless America!

Yours truly,

N.O. SLAK

PS The 28th Amendment would allow the people of the US to impeach the President because he or she does not listen to the voice of the people. Although many people did not like President Bush going to war, there was never an outpouring of criticism that can possibly compete with the people of America voicing their decent over universal health care.

Moreover, a President shall never condone his affiliated party to intimidate, harass or misguide the majority of the people. If America votes another person like you into office, whereas he or she chooses not to listen to the will of the people, the punishment shall be for them to bust rocks on the side of Interstate 14 in California.

Conclusion

I wrote this book for the silent majority. If Al Sharpton wants to be the voice for black people, then I want the job to speak for the masses and I am colorblind. I want my voice to be the clarion call for the normal people in society. I don't belong to the Tea Party, nor do I want a drastic change. I simply want people to think twice before they want immediate change.

As an example, there was some legislation passed in having guardrails changed on some of our interstates. This cost the taxpayers hundreds of millions of dollars, solely because a small group thought we needed the change. If somebody dies from hitting a tree, should we remove all the trees?

This is a waste of money! It is my money and I'm sick and tired of congressional people spending my money like a bunch of drunken Indians. Did we lose our vision as the most powerful nation in the world? The hand of God touched our country and now we have to ward off the evil spirits on a daily basis.

To name a few, we treat our military veterans, senior citizens and people that genuinely need help as if they're lepers. Who cares about non-pointy guardrails, smoking outdoors or if people are wearing mink coats? We have turned our country into a land of sniveling misfits. Who has the fortitude in congress to run on my platform? Who is going to say, "I am taking my country back!"

Although I carefully chose the words in this book, there is some logic behind my style. Although people may think I do not care about mentally impaired children, senior citizens or anybody else I may have offended, you know nothing about me. My parents, whom I love more than life itself are in their early eighties and are American heroes to me.

I have three cats and love animals immeasurably, but I do not love them over human life.

I anguished for months whether to leave the comments I wrote about drivers hitting stationary objects. My nephew died in February 2009 after his car slammed into a tree in Gainesville, FL after suffering a seizure. I miss you Jason. In fact, we all miss you. You will forever be in my thoughts. How's life in heaven? Have you told anybody to Cowboy- up?

I lost two friends in Vietnam when I was only eleven years old. They were the neighborhood teenagers who never came home. To this day, I still remember Carl and Art who were the teenagers that let me *hang out* with them. I'm sure God let them grow back their hippy hair, so they didn't have the buzz-cut forever. You were both too young, but I will never forget.

I have a retarded stepbrother (at least I think he is retarded) and I have family members with ailments. When I use the words slow or retarded, I am referring to people that choose not to use their functioning brains. Those words are not intended to hurt families that have mentally impaired family members.

A dear friend of mind is 70% blind, and will be completely blind within one year. He still plays in a band and is incredibly talented.

The reason I'm letting people know this information is that the reader should be informed about my background.

I will always continue to donate my time, heart and soul for our Vietnam Veterans, as well as all veterans. The Vietnam War Museum in Orlando Florida has become my second home.

To: PK, MURPH, KOJAK, CRAZY EDDIE, BUDDA, BLONDY RAMSEY, COLONEL PINK-DICE, PAPA-SMURF and my brother-in-law TY, I salute each of you. If I included all the names, the book would never end. Your camaraderie is endearing and something that no human or higher force can mock. You and your fallen angels prove to me that America will triumph every time we visit. When this book is completed, we are having a *beer bash and rocking the house*! ~~If President Obama cares to have a beer with us, we will show him how it is done. We will show our commander in chief respect, despite our disagreements.~~ Did I just say that? I love computers.

To my daughters, Amanda and Lynn, thanks for being true to yourselves. You have grown to become adults and now have your own families. I am proud of each of you. Do not ever ask me who my favorite is unless we are alone, but you have to promise not to tell the other. Parents always have a favorite child, but they will not reveal it in fear of a family meltdown. The difference between normal parents and me is I accept bribes.

To my sister Carole and brother Kirk, you are always in my prayers. As my niece Shannon would say, "Peace"!

To my friends, especially DONNY, JIMBO, DOO, LYLE, SCOOBY, NORBSTER, TREV-NUTS, LT TK and the rest of the gang, thanks for the good times and ~~may they continue for all of~~ we will never lose sight of each other, no matter what. No matter how destitute our country may become, we have each other. If you guys would only bathe, I would love you more, but not in a Broke Back way!

Lastly, to my wife Renee, I will love you forever. Thank you for letting me write this book in the style I chose, although you and I will always know the real me. Thanks for keeping that a secret, being my best friend and my soul mate. The only thing I ask of you is to stop calling me Tiger, because it just doesn't sound the same anymore.

On January 19, 2010, my father passed away. After spending 81 years on Earth, I'm sure he was ready to go and find something else to do. I am glad he went by my side, as opposed to looking at strangers' faces that belong to a death panel or a convalescent center. I'll love you always Dad and I'll have a book flown up to you in the next couple of months. Oh yeah, I know how you like practical jokes. The next time it rains in DC, make sure it is actually rain and not something else! That wouldn't be funny or respectful at all. You know what Dad; go for it! I will love you forever!

NO SLAK-OUT (Thanks Ryan Seacrest-And don't forget to email me)